THE
CANADIAN
FISHING TRIP

THE

CANADIAN

FISHING

TRIP

A GUIDEBOOK

by JOHN HARSCHUTZ

Barker & North Publishing
Post Office Box 692
Brookfield, Wisconsin 53008

FIRST EDITION
10 9 8 7 6 5 4 3 2 1

Publisher's Cataloging in Publication Data

Harschutz, John.
The Canadian fishing trip, a guidebook.

Includes index.
1. Fishing -- Guide-books   I. Title.

SH412   799.1   92-73117
ISBN 0-9630638-4-7

To those individuals

who, through their effort,

make it possible for fishermen

to experience the

Canadian adventure.

Contents

APPENDICES

Preface

The idea for this book developed years ago, just after I had made my first fishing trip to Canada. That trip was a true adventure. It was exciting. I wanted to go back. I also regretted not fishing Canada earlier in my life.

I felt that if I would have had more information about Canadian fishing trips, I would have made the trip much sooner than I did. I also thought there might be others, like myself, who could benefit from the things I had learned.

I had several goals in mind when I decided to go ahead with this project. I wanted to provide enough information so that someone could plan a "first-time" Canadian fishing trip. I wanted to provide information useful to both the initiate and the veteran angler. I wanted to present this material in a manner which would simplify planning both for the new and the veteran angler. And, I wanted to include the topics which affect the success of all portions of the fishing trip.

This book covers many topics which the reader may want to consider in planning a Canadian fishing trip. It is a guide. It does not teach everything there is to know about a fishing trip. There is a saying; "experience is the best teacher." Learn from your experience.

In addition to learning things about fishing you will gain knowledge about other things that are part of a fishing trip. Teamwork, organization, nature and the ecology are part of the experience. Every trip will teach you something new. This is all a part of the Canadian fishing adventure.

John Harschutz

Acknowledgements

I want to express my gratitude to Howard Hartwig for his assistance with graphics and film preparation. I want to thank Margo Matsick, Betty Hartwig and Barney and Jane Jelinski for their time spent in reviewing and editing these pages. I also want to thank those individuals who have offered me suggestions and provided me with information on book production.

WARNING - DISCLAIMER

This book is a general guide. It provides education and entertainment. It does not cover every possible situation that can be encountered in planning and executing a Canadian fishing trip. The final decision on what to do, what to take, where to go, and what to do once there is the responsibility of the reader.

Knowledge of safety requirements related to any and all forms of boating, fishing, and camping is the responsibility of the reader. This book does not intend to be a safety course in these areas.

The author and publisher take no liability nor responsibility to any person or entity with respect to any loss or injury, or allegation of loss or injury, directly or indirectly as a result of information contained in this book or omission of information from this book.

DECIDING TO GO

Chapter One

WHERE TO GO

Deciding where to go on your Canadian adventure requires some thought especially when you consider the ten provinces and two territories that make up Canada, the variety of fishing that can be found among them, and the different trips available to you.

Many considerations are taken into account in making this important decision. Your final decision will typically be based on how you want to travel, how far you want to travel, the length of your vacation, the type of facilities you are interested in staying at and the species of fish you are after. For the fishing trip that includes your family, you may want to consider additional activities. There are many fine resorts that are well suited for a family fishing adventure. Many of these facilities have activities that complement fishing activity and provide families with variety on their vacation. More and more families and couples are experiencing Canadian fishing.

This chapter will assist you in exploring a majority of the options open to you. The checklists at the end of this chapter will also be helpful to you.

Choosing a
Fishing Spot

Canada has both freshwater and saltwater fishing. Lake, river and ocean fishing opportunities abound. The variety of fish and fishing trips that these possibilities offer is fantastic.

Many choices exist for choosing a Canadian fishing spot. Resorts, outposts, camping, river trips, ocean charters or a combination of these are the major categories to choose from. A variety of choices are available from within each of these categories.

In examining these choices, many things will need to be considered.

Two items are usually paramount in making a decision. You will most likely want to find a happy balance between good fishing and comfort. You may choose to forego comfort for excellent fishing. Or, you may decide to maximize your comfort and settle for average fishing. The ideal is, of course, to have the best of both worlds.

Some of the different types of fishing trips and some of the considerations to take into account when deciding on a fishing trip are examined below.

Resorts

Canada has every type of resort imaginable. Resorts range from the very plush to those where you will be "roughing it." These resorts include resorts in wilderness areas accessible only by plane, resorts on or near major highways, resorts on lakes, rivers, those catering to ocean fishing, some situated literally on the ocean, and fishing ships. Each has its glamour and appeal and each brings with it a sense of adventure.

A resort or outpost is sometimes referred to as a "bush camp." Many veteran Canadian anglers will refer to their resort as a camp, probably because the term "camp" has a certain adventuresome ring to it. So you will most likely hear someone talking about a camp in some remote, or not so remote, place in Canada.

Because resorts generally offer so many opportunities, each should be examined individually for their merits.

Outposts

Outposts are typically cabins located at some distance from the main camp or central supply point. Resorts and some air services have outposts for rent. Many outposts are fly-ins but some can be driven to. When considering an outpost, ask if any other outposts or resorts exist on the lake, river, or in the vicinity.

A variation on the outpost is the houseboat. You might call it a moveable outpost. This unique type of adventure offers a lot of possibilities.

Camping

There are many fine fishing areas that you can drive to and camp at. Some of these are in the public park system. Others are campgrounds associated with resorts.

If you are considering a campground you may need refrigeration or freezer facilities, gasoline, groceries and ice. Check with the campground operator about the availability of these items.

Fly-in camping or camping associated with a fly-in resort is another camping possibility. With this type of trip, because of the plane's capacity, weight will be a factor. Tents, camp stoves, sleeping bags and possibly a canoe add to the total weight. Add these weights and compare it to the maximum weight limitation of your plane.

Depending on the province you are traveling to, camping permits for camping on public land may be required. Check with the appropriate information source for the province you are going to. See Information Sources in this chapter.

River Trips

There are many outfitters in Canada who rent equipment, sell maps, offer advice, get you to your starting point and pick you up at the end of your journey.

If you want to get into remote areas it is possible to fly a canoe into these areas. Some pilots will fly with canoes lashed to the thwarts of their planes. Helicopters are also used for carrying canoes. Check with outfitters in the areas you are interested in.

When going on a river trip be sure you have enough experience and are well informed on the requirements of canoe travel. It is advisable to have experienced people in your party for this type of trip. Check your library and book store for books on canoe travel. Try to talk to someone that has made the trip, even if this entails a few long distance calls. Before you depart on your trip, find out as much as you can about the area you are going to.

If your party is traveling without the assistance of an outfitter, always contact the local authorities. Tell them your schedule and approximate planned location each day you are on the river. If you are late in coming out of the bush, they will be looking for you.

Charters

Charter boats are available on both coasts, the Great Lakes and on other major waterways. If you decide on a charter, make reservations to guarantee that you get on a boat. Ask your captain what he or she supplies and what gear, clothing, food and refreshments you should bring. Ask how long you will fish, travel times to the fishing area and length of time on the water.

Considerations

Because of the variety of vacations available to the fisherman, there are many things you need to ask about before you decide whether or not a specific trip is what you want. Your vacation will be more enjoyable if you eliminate as many "surprises" as possible. You want to insure that your expectations correspond to reality. Some of the things you may want to ask about are listed in the following paragraphs. Many times the answers to your questions are contained in a brochure. You want to have your questions answered before you depart. If you do not understand an answer ask the question again, perhaps in a different way.

Your potential hosts will be very helpful. They also understand the importance of providing correct and adequate information to their customers. They realize that this makes for a more pleasant vacation for all concerned, and even though they have probably been asked the question many times before, they will generously provide you with an answer. They know that this is a very important part of their business.

Accommodations and Utilities

Across Canada the fisherman will find a variety of accommodations. They range from very luxurious to offering only the basics. Because of this variety, there are certain things to check when looking for a vacation spot.

Many fishermen visiting Canada for the first time incorrectly assume that electricity will always be available. This is not always the case. Many resorts use electrical generators which may only be turned on during certain parts of the day. Outposts may or may not have generators. Propane refrigerators and freezers are very common in the remote parts of Canada. Find out what is available and plan accordingly. Your water supply may come directly from the lake or you may have well water. If the water comes from the lake, ask how pure it is. Many locations have pure uncontaminated water. In these locations the water is usually only filtered. At some outposts, water is carried from the lake. If conditions warrant, boil your water before drinking it.

Indoor plumbing may or may not be available to you. Some resorts will have a complete plumbing system in each cabin. Other resorts may have a bathroom in each cabin and central showers. Some resorts will have a centrally located toilet and shower facility. Some resorts may have only cold water in a cabin. Find these things out ahead of time so that you are not surprised and can plan accordingly.

If you are choosing a housekeeping plan in which you supply and prepare your own food versus the American plan, where the resort provides all your meals, you will want to ask about the cooking facilities. I have found that a two burner range is adequate for a party of four. Limit your surprises by asking what is available. What type of frying pans and cooking utensils are supplied? Are there adequate plates, cups and silverware? Is there equipment available for shore lunches? Some housekeeping packages share cooking facilities with one or more cabins. You may want to inquire about procedures and schedules in this situation.

Even when some things are supplied, you may want to take along some items of your own. For example, I take my own coffee cup. It happens to be a porcelain covered metal cup which I prefer to many I have used. I also take aluminum "camping" plates with me on my trips for use on shore lunches. I then know ahead of time what I will be packing for the shore lunches.

You may be interested in the cabin floor plan. Some cabins are a single large room with bunks or beds and a kitchen area. Other cabins have separate rooms. Because these "cabins"have separate rooms, they may be referred to as cottages.

Another item that is not asked about very often is bedding. You will want to know what you will be sleeping on. Will you need to bring a sleeping bag? What about pillows? Will you need a foam pad?

Housekeeping or American Plan
Choosing the American plan saves you a lot of work but it may put you on a schedule set by the resort. If you want to stay on the water till dark, you may miss supper. Ask about the meal schedule on the American plan. Some plans offer sandwiches for the party that wants to maximize their time on the water.

Equipment Supplied
A primary consideration is equipment supplied by the resort. You will want to know what types of boats are available. You want to know the type and year of outboard motors. Ask if there are spare motors available at your location in case one of the motors breaks down. Ask if the gas is pre-mixed or if you have to mix it yourself. Are there nets, boat seats and life vests available or do you have to bring your own?

Find out what the resort policy is if you accidentally damage an outboard motor. This does not happen often, but Canadian lakes do have boulders in them and some of them tend to be just under the surface of the water in parts of the lake where you least expect them to be. Some resorts may require that you pay for the repair of a motor you damage; others will charge an insurance premium so you can avoid paying for a very costly repair. Motor repair is expensive. Know your responsibilities ahead of time so that a surprise does not ruin your trip.

Refrigeration and Freezing Facilities

Find out about refrigeration and freezer availability. I always ask this question because I do not always fillet my fish but rather bring them home whole after gutting them and removing their gills. Ask how a trophy will be preserved if you decide to keep one instead of releasing it. These questions are more crucial if you are at an outpost. Typically outpost freezer space is at a premium. If you will need ice, ask if it is available.

Services

Ask about other services available to you. Guides, live bait and fish cleaning services may be services you are interested in. Ask about retail outlets. Is there a grocery store nearby? Are licenses and lures available?

Emergencies

Ask how emergencies are handled. Is there a telephone or radio telephone available? If you are going to an outpost without a radio ask what type of emergency signal is used. Ask how emergencies at an outpost are handled and how often you are checked on.

Camp Restrictions

Ask about camp restrictions. Some resorts may request that all customers be off the water before dark. Some resorts may require that you hire a guide.

Fishing

Find out what fish species exist in the area you are fishing. If lake fishing, ask if you will need to portage to other lakes to get to different fishing.

<u>References</u>

You may want to ask your owner/operator for the phone numbers of references that live near you. Call these people and ask them about the fishing and what lures or bait they have had luck with. Most individuals you talk to will be very helpful. They may not tell you all their secrets but they will usually tell you what lures and bait have worked for them in the past as well as other helpful information.

Transportation _____

Transportation is an important consideration in planning your trip. Because transportation is related to cost and travel time, it is often a primary consideration in deciding where to go. Prior to deciding your transportation you may want to first choose your destination. Then decide on how you will get there. In many cases several modes of transportation will be used to get into a fishing spot. You might start with a commercial airline and then switch to a floatplane service or you may first drive to a float base and then board a floatplane. Driving, flying, taking the train, riding a chartered bus or a combination of these modes of travel are all options. These options are examined further in Chapter Five.

Cost _____

If you want to estimate what your trip will cost you. Ask the resort owner or outfitter how he charges for his services. Some resorts have a "package" price. Other resorts charge individually for such things as gasoline, freezer services, etc. Prices will be quoted in both Canadian and U.S. dollars. If only one price is quoted and the currency is not indicated, ask what currency the quote is in.

Information Sources_____

The information you need to help you decide where to go is readily available to you. In addition to the sources already mentioned, travel agencies, libraries, magazines, newspapers and television all offer insights into some of the opportunities for a Canadian fishing adventure. Local "fishing" or "sports" shows held annually in major metropolitan areas provide a chance for fishermen to talk directly with resort owners and operators. Magazines, covering fishing and travel, contain articles and advertisements on places to go. Each province and territory also provides information on travel and accommodations within their areas.

To get tourist information call 1-800-555-1212 and ask for the 800 number for Canadian travel information. Call this number and ask for specific information on accommodations, camping, outfitters, fish species available, length of seasons, size and possession limits and whatever else you want to know about the province or territory you are visiting. The Canadian information resources can provide answers to many questions and if they cannot answer a question they will give you a name, address and phone number of someone who can. These resources will also provide information on obtaining topographic maps, lake contour maps, navigation charts and aeronautical charts.

The information on fishing that you will receive from these sources will usually cover the province or a region within the province. If you want to know the different fish species in a more defined area you may need to make further inquiries of resorts or the Ministry of Natural Resources in the area.

The checklist at the end of this chapter will assist you in gathering the information you might be concerned about. If you do all your homework the first time, and find a spot that suits you, you will find that your information gathering for later trips becomes much easier.

On subsequent trips you will know what to ask about, and your checklists will provide a reminder. As in anything, the more information you have, the more successful you will be.

Inquiry Checklist _____

Fishing Information:
- __ Species of fish?
- __ Size of lake?
- __ Maps available?
- __ Accessibility to other lakes?
- __ Past fishing success of customers?
- __ Customer references?
- __ How bad are the insects?
- __ Is portaging required?
- __ Is live bait available?
- __ Condition of boat launches?

Flying:
- __ Weight restrictions?
- __ Cost (round trip)?

Availability of equipment:
- __ Types of boats?
- __ Type and year of outboards?
- __ Spare motors?
- __ Boat cushions?
- __ Pre-mixed or mix your own gas?
- __ Nets?
- __ Minnow buckets?
- __ Type and size of refrigerators and freezers?
- __ Cooking and shore lunch utensils?

Accommodations:

_ Housekeeping or American plan?

_ Electricity?

_ Plumbing?

_ Showers?

_ Type of beds and bedding?

_ Camp restrictions?

Services available:

_ Guides?

_ Fish cleaning services?

_ Phone/Radio-phone service?

_ Grocery store?

_ Lures for sale?

_ Licenses?

_ Ice available?

Cost:

_ What is included in the "package"?

_ What is the cost of items not included in the package?

_ What is the "damaged motor" policy?

Chapter Two

WHEN TO GO

Deciding when to go on your Canadian fishing adventure can be influenced by several factors. Picking a time to go requires coordinating the open fishing season, your vacation schedule, the weather you prefer and a preferred fish catching level. These and other factors are examined in this chapter.

Resort Openings _____

If visiting a resort is in your plans, you will find that in many parts of Canada early season slots are the first to fill up. Many customers make their reservations a year in advance, usually prior to leaving camp the year before. Try to make your reservations early. Do not be discouraged if you cannot get into "that" spot when you want. If you are really interested in a specific camp, ask the owner to contact you when there is a cancellation.

You want to have good fishing, right? Ask the resort owner or your outfitter about the fishing. He may say that early spring fishing is good but he will most likely add that the fishing is good all summer and also into the fall. The early season fisherman may have excellent fishing and then again good fishing may not begin until later in the season. Fishermen fishing the opener <u>may</u> be experiencing such things as uncomfortable weather, heavier than usual fishing pressure and possibly higher prices.

When fishing the salmon and trout runs, your decision will be affected by peak runs which are affected by water temperatures. The season may be open for quite some time but the best fishing is dependent on the runs to spawning grounds and the congregation of fish at the mouths of rivers prior to the runs. In some areas these fish are available all season and in others the runs are more pronounced. The resort owner or outfitter can tell you the approximate times for the runs. He usually only needs to look at his reservations list to see when his customers want to be on the water.

If you also enjoy hunting, you may be able to schedule a fishing trip that overlaps with a hunting season. For example, you might decide to hunt ducks in the mornings and evenings and fish for walleye during the day.

Seasonal Effects
On Fishing

The seasons of the year will affect the fishing to some degree. Some fishing will be dependent on the spawning runs which are related to seasonal changes. Some fishing will be dependent on water temperatures which are affected by the climate.

Average temperatures will generally be cooler the further north one goes. In the north the water temperatures of lakes and rivers usually do not warm as early in the year as lakes to their south. The impact this cold water has on fishing is good. Due to the cold water, food is not as abundant and with large fish populations the fish tend to feed more often and more aggressively. Of course, food supplies peak during the summer months and the fish can be affected by this abundance. I have found that, on the average, if a lake has moderate fishing pressure it will produce consistently all season long.

And do not forget winter and ice fishing. I know of some lakes that produce more fish through the ice than are caught during the summer.

Always keep in mind that, even during the "best" part of the season, fishing can be slow on some days and better on others.

Weather
Considerations

Is weather a factor? Do you want to fish when the chances of having good weather are high? In some spots you may need a snowmobile suit and mittens on opening day. In these spots the ice may not go out until the day before season opens.

I personally prefer to balance nice weather with good fishing. I will give up the early season fishing for warmer weather as long as the fishing is still good at that time of year.

Ask about the average monthly temperatures in the area you are interested in. Early season fishing may parallel mild weather or the weather can be cold.

One benefit of cooler weather is that it limits insect hatches for those areas of Canada where insects can be bothersome to the fisherman. On many of the "lake" fishing trips I have made, I have not used any repellant. However, insects can be a problem during warm weather and they are always worse after dark than during daylight hours. Your best advice for taking precautions against insects will come from the resort operator or local sources, but remember their knowledge may be relative to their area. It may be difficult for them to compare with other areas if they have not been there. During warm weather, your best bet is to be prepared. Take repellant along. If headnets are advised, as they are in some parts of Canada, take spares with you.

Water
Levels

Depending on locale, inland water levels can vary considerably from spring to summer to fall. Winter snows will affect the spring runoff. Above or below average rainfall will also affect water levels. Going from one extreme to the other, the piers on a lake could be four feet out of the water or a foot under water depending on the time of year and the amount of precipitation the area has received. Water levels may affect your fishing success. They are unpredictable and may vary from year to year. Your best resource for this information is the resort operator, outfitter or Ministry of Natural Resources.

Timing Checklist _____

___ Make reservations far enough in advance.
___ Ask about best fishing times.
___ Check on average weather in the area; average temperature and average rainfall.
___ Ask about the water levels and how it affects fishing.
___ Check on insect levels.

Chapter Three

PLANNING AS A GROUP

Planning, it has been said, can be half the fun. Good planning is also very important to a successful Canadian fishing adventure. This chapter covers some aspects of pre-trip planning. Other planning, such as that involving meal schedules and where to fish, can be tentatively planned and then finalized once your party is in camp.

Fishing and Meal Schedules

A lot of planning centers around meals, their ingredients and the tentative in-camp cooking schedule. If you have a choice of the American plan or housekeeping, the American plan may appear to be easier but do not make your decisions based totally on this point. Examine what you want from your trip and decide accordingly. If you are taking the American plan, meal planning is left to your hosts. When housekeeping, it is important to do some planning.

With housekeeping, planning will tend to become more difficult as your group gains in size. When this happens, divide these large groups into smaller groups to simplify things. For example, if a large group rents several cabins, do some planning at the cabin level. Once in camp, these separate groups will save considerable time in making decisions. This will provide more time to go after those trophies.

This "in-camp" planning usually involves deciding on the combined meal and fishing schedule. Usually the fishing plan is first outlined and then the meal schedule is planned around it. The decision of when to eat, where to eat and what to eat is then made. This topic is covered in more detail in Chapter 8.

Meal Planning _____

If you are camping or renting housekeeping accommodations, you will need to take your own food. It is important to discuss what you want to eat in camp and who among your party will bring specific food items. If your trip is still a few weeks away, write down everything and get copies to the people doing the shopping.

It may be possible to live on bread and fish during your stay but it is nice to have some variety in meals and to have those meals planned ahead of time. I have found that most fishing parties, where practical, have a main course of fish at one meal during the day. With this being the case, you need to plan on eating other dishes during your stay. You may decide to eat a light breakfast on most days, fish for a few hours, have a shore lunch of fish, fish again, and return to your cabin for a meal with a main course other than fish. Because weather will undoubtedly change any schedule you put together, it is advisable to put together a list of main meals and leave the schedule open. Let your meal schedule evolve during your stay.

A meal plan for a 5 day lake fishing trip (non-guided, housekeeping plan) might include the following meals;

Shore Lunch -- 3 of 5 days.
   (Take sandwiches the other 2 days).
Breakfast -- 2 days, scrambled eggs and ham.
Breakfast -- 3 days, light; no cooking.
Meals in camp:
   Steak and fish -- 2 days.
   Hot Ham sandwiches -- 1 day
   Hot Beef sandwiches -- 1 day
   Fish Chowder -- 1 day

The above example of a lake fishing menu only includes a shore lunch for three of five days because through experience I have found this to be an average among groups. My fishing partners and I try to maximize our time on the water as well as occasionally cooking and enjoying this traditional meal. Although the shore lunch is a little more work, because you have to take your cooking gear and utensils with you, it is well worth the effort. This type of dining is truly a memorable experience. The cooking is easy and the overall experience is truly enjoyable. On those days when we do not cook a shore lunch, and we plan on being on the water all day, we pack sandwiches.

When planning shore lunches, be aware that different areas in Canada will have different fire regulations and that the fire regulations change as moisture levels in the forest change. Always inquire about the fire regulations in the areas you are visiting.

Meal plans for river trips will be more complicated because of weight restrictions. Dry and freeze-dried foods occupy a considerable portion of the menus for these type of trips.

Party Size _____

Fishing parties can be of any size and after time you will decide if you prefer one size over another. Large groups that have been together for years have usually worked out a good system that keeps everyone happy. One advantage with a larger group is that the more unpopular camp chores can be spread between more people. Disadvantages include the preparation and planning time for large shore lunches as well as the time consuming planning of daily activities for the large group.

Pre-trip Meetings _____

Unless your group is a bunch of old salts, it is advisable to meet at least once prior to your trip and talk over, as a group, what will be happening during your excursion.

At this time you may want to ponder who will be doing certain camp duties. For example, if you are camping or housekeeping at a resort and you all get hungry, which is inevitable, you do not want to end up staring at each other wondering who is going to be the first person to grab the spatula. During planning, ask for a volunteer cook. If none surfaces, perhaps you may want to decide to take turns cooking. If no one wants to cook, you may want to consider a resort with the American plan.

Considerations of Party Members

In planning your trip decide as many things as you can before the trip starts; this includes the decision to put off deciding certain things until you are in camp. Consider the likes and dislikes of each party member. Try to pair up people with equal fishing skills. Find out who wants to fish with whom. Perhaps someone does not like to fish non-stop from 8:00 a.m. until 9:00 p.m. One party member may want to night fish. Another may want to break at noon for 2-3 hours. And yet another may want to sleep until noon, fish for three hours and then go back to playing cards. Talk these things over before you go. It will make your trip much more pleasant.

Planning the Workload

Try to plan your camp chores ahead of time. You can list all tasks that need to be done while you are in camp and then ask for volunteers. It may also be easier to decide to take turns at doing the different tasks. Whatever you decide, try to make your decisions before you leave home. If your group has been together for some time and someone new is joining the group, explain the usual routines that your group generally follows.

With the exception of shore lunch preparations, one task that usually is not shared is the cleaning and filleting of fish to take home. Unless this service is being provided by the resort, generally, everyone cleans or fillets and wraps their own fish. Fish cleaning for shore lunches is usually done by one or more people for everyone while others in the party prepare other things for the feast. Some resorts provide optional fish cleaning and packaging services. Your guide, for a fee or as part of his service, may also do this.

"Happy Camper" Suggestions

Don't let anyone get disgruntled by doing the same chore day after day. Share the chores that are fun and also the ones that are not. Always have a consensus on how the work will be done and try to reach that agreement before you get to camp. Also, do not lock yourself into an inflexible situation. You should agree that your plans are tentative and that they can change once you are in camp.

Once in camp, if there seems to be a lot of work, asking "How can I help?" is appropriate if you are not sure what needs to be done. If something isn't getting done, take the reins and set an example. Sometimes plans change once you arrive in camp. Sometimes, due to no one's fault, personalities will clash. If things do not seem to be going right, it is generally best to keep quiet, add it to your experiences, and make concessions as much as possible. If you are the type that wants to communicate what you feel is a problem, a nice way to bring this up is to offer a suggestion. In this manner you are not saying something has to change, you are only offering a thought for consideration by the group.

Communication among members of your party and within the party as a whole will make your overall trip a more rewarding experience. Remember that compatible groups do not happen overnight. They evolve over time. Understand that there will be differences. Also understand that successful trips usually indicate everyone was working together as a team.

Planning Checklist _____

Camp duties; who will do what?
- __ Dishes
- __ Cooking
- __ Driving the boat (Almost everyone will sign-up for this one.)
- __ Cleaning the fish for main meals
- __ Making the fire
- __ Gathering wood for the fire
- __ Hauling gear
- __ Maintaining the camp log book
- __ Setting up the tent

Considerations in planning;
- __ Likes and dislikes
- __ Health
- __ 100% fishing or other activities
- __ Tasks that will need to be done in camp
- __ Tasks that need to be done prior to the trip

PREPARATION

Chapter Four

WHAT TO TAKE

Some items are definitely needed on a fishing trip and others leave a question-mark in many people's minds. If you see any bush pilots walking around continuously shaking their heads, it is because of some of the gear they have had to fly in and out of the camps. It is not only the oddities but also on occasion the quantities that initiate wonderment. If you have a chance, ask a bush pilot about the strangest cargo he has ever had to fly. If he has time you will probably hear a good story.

When weight is not a factor, you can take anything that you think you might find useful. When weight and volume are a restriction you will usually find you can get by with a lot less.

Fishing Equipment

Fishing rods and reels can "make or break" a trip. You want to have good equipment and perhaps a backup or two in case a rod or reel would break. Your equipment needs are dependent on the species of fish you are after and the environment you will be fishing. Equipment will vary somewhat between ocean, Great Lakes, lake and river fishing.

Considering lake and river fishing, you will most likely take less gear on a river trip than you would take on a lake trip. For example, if you are fishing for brookies you will not need the heavier gear required for northerns. If the river you are fishing holds both small and large fish you may want to compromise and take a medium weight rod. Common fishing rod choices for lakes that hold lake trout, northerns, walleye and smallmouth are two rods, one a medium weight and the other a heavier "musky" type rod. The medium weight rod can be used for casting, for trolling smaller lures and for jigging. The heavier rod is used to troll and cast large lures for the larger fish. Taking along a light rod and reel can be a lot of fun due to the action when you hook a larger fish.

For river trips, many fishermen prefer a medium action and a light action rod and reel. If you are taking two rods on a river trip, to minimize gear, you may not want to take backups. Portaging extra gear on a river trip can make you wish you would have taken only "the bare necessities." If you are fly fishing you may want to take an extra rod tip with you.

An integral part of a rod and reel is the fishing line. I cannot over-emphasize the importance of having new line on your equipment. If your line is to break, it will likely be broken by the biggest fish you hook. To avoid losing a trophy, keep new line on all your reels. Also add line to open-face reels when the line drops noticeably below the edge of the spool. The extra drag this spool exposure causes will usually affect your casting distance, casting accuracy and drag tension.

Preference of line weight varies among fishermen. Some general quidelines in this area are 10-12 lb. test on medium weight rods and 4-8 lb. test on ultra-lights. A heavier "trolling" rod can have anything from 14 lbs on up. If you use this rod for casting larger lures you will most likely stay in the 18-30 lb. range.

Lures, leaders and other tackle are often personal choices. However, certain lures in a given area will produce better than other lures. Ask for advice from the resort owner or consult with someone that has fished the area before. Use your personal experience but always be ready to try something new.

Leaders are important especially when fishing in waters holding northern and musky. Good quality snaps are a must.

Take along a compass and get a map of the water you will be fishing. The resort or camp owner will provide a map or should be able to tell you where you can get one. If size limitations are in effect you will need a measure for measuring your fish. Check with the resort owner and see if he supplies landing nets. If he does not, take one along. Other fishing equipment that you might find necessary to include in your baggage is listed at the end of this chapter.

If possible, do tackle adjustments at home. Working on tackle in camp is usually frustrating because uses time that could otherwise be spent fishing. When the fish are hitting and your fishing partner is reeling in one after the other and you are still in the process of rigging your gear, you are going to wish you had done the rigging at home.

Clothing _____

Before my first trip to Canada, I asked the owner of the resort we were going to if he could tell me what type of weather we could expect in late June. He told me "we could expect to get all four seasons in one day."He was not exaggerating much. What he basically meant was to be prepared for any type of weather; hot, cold, wet and bright sunshiny weather.

The clothing you will take will depend somewhat on the time of year and the season in which you are vacationing. Try to be prepared for the possible extremes which can occur for the time of year you are fishing.

Rainwear

A good rain suit, jacket <u>and</u> pants, really goes a long way in making a fishing trip more comfortable. Once on the water, a fishing party does not want to return to camp because one person out of the bunch is wet and cold. Most fishermen are never without a rain suit when they are on Canadian waters. Storm fronts can move in quickly and also depart quickly and usually do not give you time to return to camp and get your rain gear. So pack it with you on those days that look like rain. On those days when the wind is brisk, your rain suit does double-duty in breaking the wind.

Outerwear

Knowing the weather extremes for the time of year you will be fishing will tell you what type of clothing you should take. Many times you will be experiencing nice weather interspersed with uncomfortable weather. It is always easy to shed garments if it becomes warm. It may not be as easy to keep warm if you have not packed warmer clothing.

For fishing in extremely hot and sunny weather, take along a light long sleeve shirt to protect your arms from sunburn. For cool weather take clothing that can be layered; long underwear, a flannel shirt or two, a heavier cotton shirt and a sweater or vest. For cold weather fishing you may want to consider taking woolen trousers, one or two wool shirts and a couple of pair of wool socks. If very cold weather is expected, you may want to take a winter coat, gloves and heavier woolen socks.

Warm outdoor garments are made from many different fabrics. For colder weather, I personally prefer to wear wool because water does not evaporate from wool as quickly as it does from some other materials. Chilling of one's body is due to evaporation of water from your clothing. Evaporation requires heat and that heat is taken from your body. If your body cannot replace that warmth, you become chilled. In an emergency situation where your clothing is wet, you may be able to stay warmer longer if you are dressed in woolens or some material offering the same or greater protection against evaporation that wool offers.

To be safe, wear a life jacket when wearing heavy clothing. If you accidently end up in the water, heavy wet clothing would make swimming impossible. For comfort, less bulky shirts and jackets will wear better under a life jacket.

Footgear

For safety reasons, rubber soled shoes or their equivalent are typically worn on boats. These shoes offer better traction on potentially slippery surfaces.

When boating, a pair of light high-top rubber boots will keep your feet dry during and after a rain. These easily fold up and are quickly pulled on over your shoes. In very warm weather, many fishermen wear jogging or tennis shoes. Packing two pair allows swapping the wet with the dry pair. If, on your trip, all your footwear gets wet and you cannot get it dried out due to the cool damp weather, try wearing plastic bags over a pair of dry socks. Bread bags work well for this. The plastic between your dry socks and wet shoes should keep your feet warmer than if you wore wet shoes with no water barrier.

In cold weather, depending upon your tolerance to cold, you may need an insulated boot.

When stream and river fishing with hip boots or waders, consider using felt soles. The felt provides for better traction on slippery surfaces. Ask your hosts for information on this before you leave home.

Headgear

You will appreciate a good fishing hat. A hat that has a large bill works well. A dark colored cloth on the underside of the bill aids in cutting down on reflected light bouncing off the water. A good hat coupled with a pair of good sunglasses improves visibility considerably on bright sunny days.

You can experience cool days even during the warmest months. I always pack a wool watch cap. I have rarely used it during the warmest summer months but when I did need it, I was thankful I had it with me. A watch cap can also be worn at night to keep you warm. It is estimated that fifty percent of heat loss from the body occurs through the head area. If you are cold, this is a good area to cover.

Insects and Sun

Long sleeve shirts are a necessity for protection from the sun and from insects.

A light long-sleeve cotton shirt will protect your arms from further sunburn on those days when there is not a cloud in the sky. If necessary, the collar on the shirt can be turned up to further protect your neck area.

Depending on your destination and the time of year, insects could be bothersome. A tightly woven, heavy cotton shirt can prove invaluable against biting insects. Sometimes headnets or the newer insect proof jackets with headnet hoods are taken along as an added measure of protection. Inquire of the information sources in the area you will be visiting.

Cooking Equipment
& Eating Utensils _____

Find out what the resort supplies. Given the multitude of resort owners, you will find a variety of opinions from these very well meaning people as to what you need. Ask what they supply and then decide if you need to take additional items.

For shore lunches, if shore lunch kits are not supplied, take along something to transport your frying pan, plates, spatula, silverware, salt shaker and food. A small duffle bag or backpack works well for this purpose.

If you plan on cooking over a wood fire a small container of charcoal lighter proves helpful in starting the fire. Instead of trying to level pans using rock supports, I have found a small wire grate works well in keeping pans level over the fire. If one is not supplied I take one wrapped in newspaper and secured with rubber bands to prevent it from getting any other baggage dirty.

Always check the fire restrictions for your area. If there are restrictions on open camp fires, take a camping stove. Use of a camping stove will also save you cooking time. The trade-off is the additional weight of the stove and the space the stove takes.

Even when some things are supplied, you may want to take some items of your own. For example, a favorite coffee cup of mine is always on my list. If you have a favorite spatula you use for camping or a favorite frying pan you may want to include these in your baggage. Paper plates may also make cleanup easier. Camper's silverware kits might be something else you would find more convenient than using the silverware supplied by the resort, camp or outfitter. I like to take aluminum "camping" plates with me for use on shore lunches if these are not supplied. I then know ahead of time what plates I will be packing for the shore lunches. These added conveniences can make a trip more pleasurable. Make your decisions on taking these items after talking to your hosts.

Also take along a small cooler. Use it for stowing your beverages and snacks for the day. At the end of the day, this cooler can then be used to hold your cleaned fish.

Other Equipment

You may need to take your own dish cleaning supplies. One or two metal scrubbing pads come in handy. One or two dish towels and a dishcloth may be needed if you are "housekeeping." A clothesline will prove its worth. And each person should have a knife for filleting fish.

Fish wrapping supplies will include plastic bags, masking tape and a waterproof marking pen. Take one large cooler and one small cooler for every two people. If you are housekeeping, the coolers can be used to haul in your frozen food. You will need coolers to haul out your frozen fish.

In areas that are not overly warm, a burlap bag can be useful in stowing the day's catch until you can clean or fillet your fish later in the day. This method eliminates the need to pull in a stringer or basket each time you move to a new fishing spot. The bag must be kept wet. If the bag is kept wet the fish will be kept cool through evaporation. This bag should be kept out of the sun and placed where the air can get to it. Placing fish on ice after they are caught is even a better method of preserving your catch. This requires a larger cooler and a supply of ice.

Buoys are sometimes used to mark where fish are caught. A buoy can be made using any clear plastic bottle. Spray the inside of the bottle with orange fluorescent paint and attach a line and weight.

Bait

For freshwater fishing, the most commonly used live bait are minnows, leeches and nightcrawlers. Minnows are a good bait but require more maintenance than leeches and nightcrawlers. Leeches and nightcrawlers are easier to transport than minnows. When transporting bait, and while you are in camp, keep your bait in a cool place.

There are restrictions on taking certain live bait across the U.S. Canadian border. Check with your information sources before you leave home.

Food

Canada has some restrictions on the amount of food an individual can bring into the country. Check with your information sources prior to your trip and find out what the limitations are. If you plan on buying food in Canada, ask about the availability of stores in the area you are visiting and do not wait until the last minute to make any important purchases. Also check the Canadian holidays. They differ from U.S. holidays. Stores may be closed on certain major Canadian holidays.

Packing Suggestions

When transporting rods and reels, take the reels off the rods. Put the rods in rod cases or tie the rods together with ties so that the combined strength of all of the rods protects each rod. When doing this, secure each rod tip to a larger rod so that the tip does not easily catch on something and break. You are asking for trouble if you do not protect your rods in some manner. Reels should also be protected in some way. Put them in your tackle box or wrap them in clothing and put them in your clothes bag.

Use duffle bags rather than hard-shelled suitcases. Duffle bags stow much more easily, especially in bush planes. Do not leave a lot of small items unpacked. Rather, pack them together in something larger. If cardboard boxes are used, tape or tie the boxes shut.

Pack items that will be used during the trip in an easily accessible duffle bag. Keep your camera where you can get at it quickly. There always seem to be photographic opportunities that require taking a quick picture. Also have your rain gear handy. Have a sheet of plastic handy in case your gear happens to be sitting on a runway or on a pier when a rainstorm begins. A poncho works well for this purpose.

Pack things in such a way that minimizes searching for and repacking things once in camp. For example, if you take a small bag with you in the boat, then pack those items in that bag at home. Once in camp you will not have to go through several bags looking for and repacking that gear.

Instead of carrying all extra fishing gear and seldom used fishing lures in your tackle box, pack these items separately and only access them when you need them. I use a small plastic tackle box without shelves which also works well for packing backup reels. This also allows me to carry a smaller and lighter tackle box.

Plastic milk jugs filled with water, frozen and placed in coolers with frozen food will keep these foods frozen longer. Once in camp this source of ice, placed in a cooler, will keep live bait fresh for some time during warm weather. After the ice thaws, the plastic jugs can be cut in such a way as to make a boat bailer or a funnel, if needed.

Pack sleeping bags inside one or two plastic bags to keep them dry. Once wet, a sleeping bag is very heavy and also difficult to dry out, especially in damp weather.

Weight Restrictions _____

If you are restricted by a weight limitation, weigh all your gear. An easy way to do this for items that do not easily sit on a scale is to stand on a scale, take a reading of your weight, pick up whatever baggage you are weighing, take another reading and subtract the two readings. The difference will be the weight of the item.

Some of your heavier items will be those which contain water. For example a case of beer or soda in aluminum cans weighs between twenty and twenty-three pounds. A gallon of water weighs between eight and nine pounds.

Optimize on tackle and clothing. Take a smaller tackle box. Review your selection of lures. Find out which lures work and take several replacements. If you have a tendency to lose lures or your host says there are a lot of snags, take extras. Travel in your fishing clothes if weight restrictions are really tight.

Packing Checklist _____

The following lists include many "optional" items. Some items are necessary while others can be left behind, especially if weight or capacity is a limitation. Some items may be supplied by the resort or outfitter.

After each fishing trip review your list and add or delete items. You will find that different types of trips will develop different lists. By creating a checklist for each type of trip you will save valuable time in preparing for future trips.

This list is not all inclusive. There may also be items not mentioned in these lists that you feel are a very necessary part of your gear.

Regarding food, Chapter 12 contains an "example" list of food items to take.

Fishing Equipment:

___ Rods, reels and tackle box(es)

___ Small "tackle-box" scale

___ Small measure

___ Fillet knife and/or jackknife

___ Knife sharpening stone

___ Compass

___ Lake maps

___ Landing net

___ Waterproof matches or lighter

___ Insect repellant

___ Fishing vest

___ Bait and containers for use in boat

___ Live basket, stringer and/or burlap bag

___ Needle-nose pliers

___ Wire mouth spreader

___ Barometer

___ Fish locator

___ Large cooler

___ Small cooler

___ First-aid kit and manual

___ Signal mirror

___ Flashlight, extra bulb and batteries

___ Rope

___ Duct tape

___ Fish marker buoys

___ Collapsible bucket

___ Fishing regulations and license

___ Thermometer

___ Combination padlock

___ Fish cleaning glove

___ Fish skinning tool

___ Fish cleaning board

__ Handwarmers
__ Waders/hip boots
__ Extra bail springs
__ Tool kit to include but not limited to:
combination screwdriver, chrome wire, small blade
screwdriver, pliers and a small tube of glue

Equipment for Boat:
__ Boat cushions
__ Life-jackets
__ Boat seats
__ Bailing device or large sponge
__ Sea anchor

Packaging Supplies:
__ Plastic bags
__ Masking tape
__ Marker pen

Outpost/Cabin Equipment (dependent on accommodations):
__ Sleeping bag wrapped in plastic
__ Air mattress
__ Clothesline
__ Lantern and fuel/batteries
__ Newspaper for starting stove fire
__ Insect spray to spray out cabin

Camping Equipment:
__ Insect proof and waterproof tent
__ Cook tent
__ Rain fly
__ Ground sheet
__ Sleeping bags
__ Cots, air or foam mattress'

Camping Equipment, continued:

__ Cooking equipment (see below)

__ Dish washing pans

__ Table cloth and tacks

__ Lawn chairs

__ Clothesline

__ Lantern and fuel/batteries

__ Small broom

__ Door mat

__ Hatchet, axe and/or saw

__ Fire starting fluid and matches

__ Rope

__ Electric cord if electric is available

__ Hose if tap water is available

Cooking Equipment (housekeeping, camping
                    & shore lunch):

__ Stove and fuel

__ Recipes

__ Matches or lighter

__ Fry pan(s) and small spatula

__ Medium sized kettle

__ Coffee pot

__ Cutting board (dependent on recipes)

__ Aluminum plates and/or paper plates

__ Cups

__ Forks and spoons

__ Closing butter dish

__ Salt and pepper shakers

__ Can opener

__ Plastic garbage bags

__ Dish soap and dish scrubber

__ Dish cloth and dish towels

___ Paper towels
___ Folding wire "basket" grill
___ Fire grate
___ Fire starting fluid
___ Hatchet and/or axe and/or saw
___ Pack for carrying shore lunch gear

Clothing:
___ Rain suit; pants and jacket with hood
___ Fishing hat
___ Wool hat
___ Heavy flannel shirt
___ Light flannel shirt(s)
___ Light long-sleeve cotton shirt for
    protection on hot sunny days
___ Wool shirt
___ Pants and belt
___ Underwear and long underwear
___ Socks
___ Light wool socks
___ Water-proof footwear or light rubber boots
___ Jogging or tennis shoes
___ Swim suit or shorts

For colder weather you may want to include
one or more of the items below:

___ Wool pants
___ Insulated vest
___ Heavy jacket
___ Heavy wool socks
___ Wool sweater
___ Winter-type boots
___ Wool or insulated gloves

Personal Gear:

- __ Birth, baptismal or voter's certificate
- __ Shaving kit
- __ Mirror
- __ Towel, washcloth
- __ Toilet paper
- __ Polarized sunglasses
- __ Extra eyeglasses
- __ Sunscreen
- __ Lip salve
- __ Hand lotion
- __ Insect repellent
- __ Two insect head nets (if necessary)
- __ Insect jacket with hood
- __ Alarm clock
- __ Credit cards/travelers checks/cash
- __ Itinerary (leave a copy at home)
- __ Important phone numbers
- __ Camera, film and flash
- __ Binoculars
- __ Pocket knife
- __ Notebook and pen
- __ Toothpicks
- __ Candy
- __ Beverages
- __ Thermos bottle
- __ Playing cards

Car Items:

- __ Road maps
- __ Insurance Card
- __ Spare key(s)
- __ Tool kit

__ Flares
__ Chain, tow strap or winch
__ "SEND HELP" sign
__ Tire repair kit and tire pump
__ Spare fuses, belts, hoses
__ Jumper cables
__ Spare tire, jack & lug wrench

Chapter Five

HOW TO GET THERE

In planning your trip, you will want to consider how you will travel to
that hotspot. Usually your decisions will be influenced by three factors;
distance, time and cost. Obviously, different modes of travel require
different schedules and usually the quicker you get there the more it
will cost you. For example, air fares generally cost more than driving
costs. This chapter examines the primary modes of transport used in
getting into camp.

Transportation _____

Driving

There are many fine fishing spots in Canada that you can drive to.
This type of transportation is usually the most reasonable in terms of
cost. Driving the entire way allows you to take as much gear as you
can pack in (and on) your vehicle. This mode of transportation also
allows you to take your own boat and motor. Many fisherman choose
a spot that they can drive to, while others will drive a majority of the
way and then transfer to another conveyance such as a boat, a train or
a bush plane.

If you are driving to a remote area, you may want to check with the
Canadian authorities in that area regarding the area's road conditions.

One word of caution when driving in moose country at night, be
alert. Moose are black and at night they are difficult to see.

Flying

Flying is usually the only way to get into many spots. If you elect to fly,
this type of transportation will add to the excitement of your
adventure. Resorts will sometimes have their own planes and will fly

you into their main camp or to their outposts. If they do not do their own flying, they will employ a flying service or tell you of flying services in the area which you can then contact. Many flying services also have outposts which they rent and fly you to as part of a package.

If you are flying with a flying service, make reservations with them well in advance of your vacation and then confirm your reservations closer to your departure date. Give an approximate time for your arrival at the float base and then make every effort to be there on time.

Flying schedules are usually somewhat flexible. If the base has a busy day, the schedule will be tighter. In these cases your arrival time at the float base is more crucial. To keep the majority of their customers happy, the flying service will attempt to stay on schedule. If you are late, they will most likely not delay others by waiting for you.

If you have made reservations, they will be expecting you and if you are on time they will get you and your gear on board and in the air in short order. If they have had bad weather, they may be trying to get back on schedule and you may have to wait for a plane.

When you fly, the amount of gear you take is limited by weight and volume restrictions. You will need to know, approximately, what you and your gear weigh. The resort owner or your flying service will tell you the plane's weight and volume restrictions. After you know this, you can decide what, if anything, you will leave behind.

If you feel that you absolutely need more gear than the weight and volume restrictions allow, the flying service or the camp owner, if he is flying you, will probably be able to fly in your extra gear on a second flight. Verify that this can be done before you leave home. This will usually entail an extra charge. You may also have to wait for that second flight because of daylight, the pilot's schedule, weather, etc.

Camp owners and flying service personnel are continuously amazed at all the "extra" equipment they transport in and out of the Canadian bush. If necessary, you can probably find something to leave behind. Take tackle, for example. I believe a person can get by with a cigar box of tackle. In fact, many canoeists do just that.

When flying remember that occasionally weather conditions can affect your arrival and departure times. "Bush" flying is done during the day and requires a certain amount of visibility. If weather is not suitable for flying you will have to wait until it clears. Check with your flying service regarding potential weather problems. Each part of Canada is affected differently by the weather. Depending on the front and the location you are at, the foul weather may move through very quickly or it may stay around longer. Ask about potential flying delays.

Train

The train in Canada also provides a means of getting into and out of fishing areas bordering the train line. Train travel in some cases provides an alternative to flying into some camps. Check train schedules and stops with both the Canadian rail information sources and the resort or outfitter you are interested in.

The train also offers another way of getting into a starting point of a river trip. In the past, a fishing party could take their canoe on the train as part of their baggage and then ask the train to stop at an unscheduled stop. The train could then be hailed when the party wanted to board. Because rules and regulations are continuously changing, check with the rail lines regarding canoe transport and unscheduled stops before you start any serious planning. Railroad information numbers can usually be obtained through the provincial or territorial tourist information offices.

Charter Bus

Another mode of travel is the bus charter. Some Canadian resorts have charters which will provide bus transportation from major hubs in the U.S. and Canada to their resorts. Some travel agencies will also provide packages.

Commercial Air

Sometimes, due to distance, the only option open to the fisherman is to fly commercial. Many times the commercial flyer will have to transfer to a smaller "bush" plane to get into camp. Many resorts will offer transportation to and from a commercial airport in their area. This eliminates the need to rent a car upon arrival at the airport.

Travel in Canada

Travel in Canada requires that you have automobile insurance, some knowledge of the metric system in order to obey speed limits and knowledge of some general traffic laws.

When driving in Canada, take a Canadian Non-Resident insurance card with you. Your insurance agent can provide this to you.

Gasoline in Canada is measured in liters at the gas pump. There are approximately 3.78 liters to one gallon. To calculate U.S. gallons, divide total liters pumped by 3.78. The result is U.S. gallons. Divide this into the cost. The result of this division is the cost of a gallon of gas in Canadian dollars. Most major credit cards are accepted in Canada.

Distances in Canada are measured in kilometers. One kilometer equals approximately .6 of one mile. To calculate miles, multiply kilometers by .62 Speed limits are in kilometers per hour. A speed limit sign of 100 Km/h is equal to 60 miles per hour (100 x .6).

Time zones may be different in Canada. So that this does not inadvertently affect your schedule, check on this if you are on a tight schedule.

Laws governing such things as seat belts and radar detectors are different in the different provinces and territories. For example, possession of a radar detector is illegal in the territories and several of the provinces. Check with the tourist information resource for the province or territory you are visiting before you leave home. Ask specifically for the *Canada Travel Information* brochure. This brochure contains a lot of information on customs regulations, duties on goods and similar travel information.

Travel Checklist _____

__ Canadian Non-Resident Insurance Card
__ Road maps
__ Weight of people plus gear
__ Reservations
__ Travel distances and travel times
__ Itinerary (leave a copy at home)

Chapter Six

BORDER & FISHING REGULATIONS

Fishing Regulations _____

Each Canadian province and territory has different fishing regulations. It is very important that you know and follow the fishing regulations for the area you are fishing. An otherwise fun filled vacation could easily be ruined by a fine and confiscation of your catch. Barbless hooks, single hooks, slot-size limits, and catch and release are showing up more and more in fishing regulations. Regulations can cover an entire province, territory or a more specific region within these areas and can usually be obtained prior to your trip. Many sport/vacation shows, stateside, have a Canadian booth at them. These booths often have regulations to hand out for the provinces and territories closest to you. You can also write or call the Canadian information source for the province or territory you are fishing (see Chapter 1).

Find out where you can obtain a fishing license. Many times your resort owner will have fishing licenses for sale. Sport shops and certain government offices also have licenses for sale. If you plan on purchasing your license at a government office remember that these offices will usually not be open on weekends. Many places of business will not be open on major Canadian holidays. These holidays do not coincide with holidays in the U.S., so plan accordingly. If for some reason you will have difficulty buying a license in Canada, check with a Canadian Ministry of Natural Resources office. You may be able to purchase your license through the mail.

Depending on the species of fish you are fishing for, you may be required to purchase stamps in addition to the fishing license. These stamps are usually then affixed to your license. Licenses can usually be purchased for different time spans varying costs. Special fishing permits are required to fish in all Canadian National Parks.

For provinces and territories bordering the ocean, saltwater and freshwater fishing may require separate licenses.

Border Regulations _____

When you enter Canada, you are entering a foreign country which has its own laws. Fortunately, these laws are very similar to those in the United States. Canadian laws place restrictions on what can be brought into Canada and similarly the U.S. has laws governing what can be brought into the U.S. from Canada. These restrictions are called border regulations. Among these are regulations governing food amounts, transportation of bait, amount of liquor and cigarettes, value of gifts, import of agricultural products and firearms. If you are unaware of the regulations, you may find yourself leaving things at the border or paying an unexpected duty. The Canadian Government provides a pamphlet entitled *Canada Travel Information* which covers many of these restrictions. Ask for this pamphlet when you contact the information source for the province or territory you are planning on visiting.

When crossing the border going into Canada and returning to the U.S. you will be asked questions by the border guards. The border guards also have the right to search you and your vehicle for illegal materials.

The *Canada Travel Information* brochure states, at the time of this writing, that "citizens or legal, permanent residents of the United States do not require passports or visas" to cross into Canada. It also states "to assist officers in speeding the crossing, and particularly to re-enter the U.S.A., native-born U.S. citizens should carry some identification papers showing their citizenship, such as a birth, baptismal or voter's certificate." Although this is stated in the brochure, the border guards do not always ask for this identification.

Boats and motors are considered personal baggage when brought into Canada.

Regulations Checklist _____

___ Inquire about fishing regulations in the province or territory where you plan on fishing.

___ Know the border regulations prior to crossing the border.

___ Consider taking a birth, baptismal, or voter's certificate.

Chapter Seven

EXPENSES & CANADIAN CURRENCY

Prior to a trip that includes several people try to decide how you will pay for and record the expenses of the trip. Keep in mind that you want to keep your bookkeeping as simple, accurate and fair as possible. The following paragraphs will give you some insight on how to do this.

Different Systems

There are many different ways of paying for the various costs of your fishing trip. Your group may elect to have one person collect money and take care of all expenses. You may decide to pay for some things individually and pay for the remainder of expenses from a fund that everyone contributes to. Or you may decide to let each party member pay for certain expenses out-of-pocket and calculate individual charges after your trip.

Whatever method you choose, it is important to a successful trip that you account for your expenses. By listing your costs and providing all members of the group with a copy of the list, you record valuable information for planning future trips. If individuals pay money into a fund or pay for expenses individually for use by the whole group then those amounts should also be recorded.

An Example

The following example illustrates one method of accounting for expenses. It is simple, fast, fair and accurate. It allows anyone to pay for any purchases the group feels they should make. It is fast in that it requires only that the purchase, and who paid for it, be recorded. After the trip is over the costs can be calculated and divided equally among all group members.

With this method, if someone in the group does not use something, they can be left out of the billing. For example, if one person decides to bring his own bait and the rest of the party buys bait as a group, this method provides a fair way of dividing the costs among the individuals using the purchased bait.

An example work sheet for this type of accounting follows. In this example Allen drove his vehicle a portion of the way and paid for all the gas. He had a flat tire and the rest of the party decided to buy him a new tire since he had volunteered the transportation. Al paid for the tire on his charge card. George paid for all the food. Both Bill and Duane paid a portion of the plane's fuel bill. Duane, the pilot, drinks scotch. He purchased the beer but he does not owe anything since he is not going to drink any of it. George knows a biologist who gave him some "secret" bait so he did not want any leeches. Duane also paid for the leeches.

Cost for any item is divided among the individuals using the item and the amount is written in the "owes" column under their name. At the end of the trip, columns are totaled. Differences between what has been paid and what is owed determines if the person has money coming or owes money. In this example, Allen and Duane each paid more than their share of expenses. They are reimbursed by Bill and George.

The cost to each person is found in the TOTAL line under the 'owes' column. Allen's cost was $128, Duane's was $136, Bill paid $145 and the trip cost George $141.

	ALLEN paid	ALLEN owes	DUANE paid	DUANE owes	BILL paid	BILL owes	GEORGE paid	GEORGE owes
GAS	$80	$20		$20		$20		$20
TIRE	51			17		17		17
FOOD		25		25		25	$100	25
FUEL		70	$160	70	$120	70		70
BAIT		4	12	4		4		
BEER		9	27			9		9
TOTAL	131	128	199	136	120	145	100	141
diff.	−3		−63		25		41	
	128	128	136	136	145	145	141	141

Balancing check: 25 + 41 −3 −63 = 0

Canadian Dollars and
Currency Exchanges _____

To save time, convert your U.S. dollars to Canadian dollars at a U.S. bank prior to your trip. Since some banks do not offer this service, call first. Exchange rates can vary between banks. You can save a few dollars by shopping around.

If you cannot get to a U.S. bank that offers this service, exchanges, banks and retailers in Canada will exchange Canadian currency for U.S. dollars. Check to see where you can get the best exchange rate.

Whenever you convert money you pay a conversion fee which is included in the exchange rate.

Calculating the
Exchange Rate _____

An "exchange rate" is the ratio of the value of money between two countries. The exchange rate is usually stated in reference to the country you are in. If you are in the U.S., the exchange rate is stated in reference to what a Canadian dollar would cost in U.S. dollars. For example, if the exchange rate in a U.S. bank is .875, each Canadian dollar will cost you 87.5 cents. If you want to find out how many Canadian dollars you will receive for your U.S. dollars, divide the U.S. dollar amount by the rate ($100 U.S. divided by .875 = $114.00 Canadian). The lower the U.S. exchange rate, the more Canadian dollars you will receive.

When in Canada, the exchange rate is typically stated in reference to what a U.S. dollar would cost in Canadian dollars. If the "exchange" in Canada is 1.14, a U.S. dollar is worth $1.14 in Canadian currency. In other words, that U.S. dollar buys $1.14 of Canadian money.

Once you know the U.S. exchange rate it is helpful to know what exchange rate in Canada is equivalent to the U.S. exchange rate. This knowledge can save you money when you are in Canada and when you have the option of paying for things in either U.S. dollars or Canadian dollars. For example, if you paid a U.S. exchange rate of .85 for your Canadian money, the equivalent Canadian rate would be 1.18. If a resort or merchant in Canada would offer a higher Canadian rate than 1.18 you could save money by using your U.S. dollars instead of your Canadian dollars.

To calculate an equivalent exchange rate, divide the exchange rate into 1. For example, with a U.S. exchange rate of .875, the equivalent rate in Canada would be 1.14 (1 divided by .875). If an exchange, store or bank in Canada would give you a higher rate than 1.14, then you would be getting more Canadian dollars for your U.S. dollar than you would get stateside at the .875 U.S. exchange rate. The table below gives the equivalent exchange rate in terms of each countries exchange rate. At the time you buy your Canadian money calculate the equivalent exchange rate and note it somewhere where it is easy to reference.

Equivalent Exchange Rates

U.S.	Canada
1.00	1.00
.95	1.05
.90	1.11
.85	1.18
.80	1.25

This equivalency table only assists you in determining where you are getting a better exchange, in the U.S. or Canada. It is not used in converting dollars once you are in Canada.

Canadian Purchases
in U.S. Dollars _____

Many travelers use U.S. dollars when they are in Canada. It sometimes helps to know how to price an item in terms of U.S. dollars. An example will illustrate the arithmetic used in calculating the U.S. dollar cost of an item priced in Canadian dollars.

If you are purchasing an item priced at $3.75 Canadian using U.S. dollars and the exchange rate is 1.25 (the Canadian exchange rate) divide the cost ($3.75) by the exchange rate. Dividing $3.75 by 1.25 equals $3.00 U.S. This is your cost if you pay for the item in U.S. dollars.

Not all divisions will divide as evenly as this example did. In most cases you need a calculator or you can ask a clerk to give you the price in U.S. currency.

IN CAMP

Chapter Eight

CAMP LIFE

You are on schedule. Your travel plans were accurate. You have now arrived in camp. You are sure about two things; you are going to fish and you are going to enjoy your trip. You have planned to remain flexible regarding the tasks required to accomplish those two goals. You have made tentative plans on how you thought things would occur once in camp. Remain flexible and let your fishing trip evolve from this point.

The information provided in this chapter should help you use your time effectively, thereby allowing more time for fishing and relaxing. Although this chapter focuses primarily on lake fishing, the ideas presented can be applied to both river and ocean fishing.

Arrival

Unless you are using an independent flying service to get into an outpost, you will normally be met by one or more of your hosts upon arrival at your destination. You may already know them from a previous visit or you may have met them at a show booth near home. If it is your first visit, your hosts will spend time with you to ensure you get properly familiarized with your surroundings. You will find them to be very helpful. Because of your previous inquiries, the camps accommodations and facilities should meet with your expectations. If some things are new to you, ask about them. If you have been to the camp before, and you want to go over some things you are unsure of, let your hosts know so that they can set aside extra time from their typically busy schedule.

If you are flying to an outpost, be sure to get your fishing licenses before you leave. If your host has not said anything about the outpost, ask if there are any specific things you need to know about the camp. Every spot has one or more things that are a little different than other camps. Also confirm emergency procedures, the time of any fly-by checks and your fly out time. Check on the location of the fish cleaning area. If maps are available, ask your host to point out some good fishing spots.

Setting up Camp - Resorts & Lodges _____

When you first arrive at camp there are always some preliminary things that need to be taken care of. After you get your gear stowed, your first order of business is to check out the fishing equipment supplied by the resort or lodge.

If you will be fishing with a boat and motor, check these out. Run the motor and if you will be trolling, check that it idles smoothly at a low rpm. If your hosts allow, tie a tag to your boat indicating it is the one you will be using during your stay. It is beneficial to use the same boat and motor for the entire stay because even though your equipment may be in top operating condition there will still be differences between equipment. Do not be surprised if your boat has no oars. Many establishments provide a large paddle which provides adequate propulsion. Any trolling is done using the motor.

If you are staying in a cabin, check that everything is operational. Your electricity may come from a generator. If it does, ask if the generator is turned off at certain times. Ask about the source of the drinking water. Lake water in many places is pure enough that drinking water is taken directly from the lake. It may be safe to drink this water but if you do not want to run any risks, boil your water before drinking it. If you have a wood stove for heating, find out where the woodpile is and, if necessary, stock up on firewood. Get your fishing license if you have not already done so. If you have a guide or would like to hire one find out how you contact the guide. Find out about camp rules. For example, camps are usually very strict about where garbage is placed and where fish are cleaned. Ask where the fish cleaning area is. Check on the water routes. If lake or ocean fishing, review the lake maps or charts with the camp operator and inquire about the fishing spots. Find out about underwater obstructions and if they are marked. Ask about fire restrictions in the area. If you are on the American plan, get the meal times.

Setting up Camp - Outposts _____

If you are flying into an outpost and you have limited communication with the main camp, someone should do a camp check before your pilot leaves. If your pilot does the check, you can assist him at this time and also get instructions from him on the operation of any unfamiliar equipment. Things commonly checked are the refrigeration, propane supply, gasoline supply and outboard operation.

Some operators hire a person to operate an outpost for the summer. These individuals live at the camp. They maintain the camp, cook for American plans and sometimes guide.

A Typical Day
on the Water _____

Getting all your gear in the boat is the first priority of the day. This task is made somewhat simpler if you put your loose items in a duffle bag. Such things as a rainsuit, jacket or shirt, camera, binoculars, flashlight and the like can all be stowed in this bag and easily transported. If your boat is some distance from your cabin you will want to minimize your trips between boat and cabin. Take a small cooler for refreshments. If you are skipping the shore lunch, the cooler can hold your sandwiches. Use the cooler at the end of the day to hold your cleaned fish prior to packaging.

If the lake is new to you, keep yourself orientated using a map and compass. While traveling on the lake occasionally reference your map and take a compass bearing so that you get some idea as to where you are located on the lake at that time.

Around lunch time start looking for a suitable lunch area on the shore. Pick a spot that is not too sheltered. Any wind will keep the insects out of the area. When cleaning up after lunch, if you have a choice, it is easier to just rinse off your dishes and then wash them back at camp. This practice is also easier on the ecology. You may notice that any soap used in washing dishes in the lake has a detrimental effect on the nearby aquatic life.

After a shore lunch, when your body has calmed somewhat from the excitement of fishing, sit back and just listen to the music of nature. Listening to the breezes pushing through the trees while resting in a sunny location can be very relaxing. Resting near and listening to a brook, rapids or waterfall can have the same effect. Take time to enjoy the serenity of your surroundings.

And always have your camera ready. Be ready for the unexpected. There are many photographic opportunities that last only a brief amount of time.

Planning Around
the Weather

Weather is usually the major item affecting your camp schedule. It will determine when and where you will fish. It dictates when to go out and when to come in. It may prevent you from fishing at some distant spot.

On days when clouds are forming and a storm is approaching, stay alert to the changing weather. Be prepared to allow enough time to get safely back to camp prior to the arrival of the storm. Do not risk your safety by fishing when it is thundering and lightning. Lightning will take the easiest path to water or ground. If you are 3 feet higher than the surrounding water you are the easiest path. If you are caught in a lightning storm, get off the water. Go to shore and stay away from any open areas and trees that are taller than the surrounding trees. If it gets close to dark and the storm continues, do not go on the water. It is better to stay overnight than to risk injury or death by being on the water. If you are familiar with the area and the sky eventually clears, you may be able to navigate at night. This, however, is not recommended if you need to traverse any type of moving water. Plan for these possible situations as a group, so that if you do not return to camp on a stormy day, the rest of the group will know you are "camping." You will rarely be in a situation that requires you to stay overnight due to lightning but you should be ready for this possibility.

Telltale signs of an approaching storm which contains lightning are black clouds and the sound of thunder. If you cannot judge which way those clouds are traveling, head for camp. If you are in a river channel away from the main lake you will not see those clouds as early as if you are on a large body of open water. In this case you have less time. So get out of there as fast as you can. If you have a smaller size outboard, an approaching storm will many times move faster than your boat. Plan for this situation. Do not take a chance. Head for home or for a safe location and come back out after the storm passes. Many times you will find a very good fishing spot close to camp on these potentially dangerous days.

Rainy days are not the same as stormy days. On rainy days you can stay on the lake as long as there is no threat of lightning. The thunder, and sometimes this will only be a rumbling sound, is usually your signal to be wary.

Fishing and
Meal Schedules _____

Your party may vote to concern itself more with the fishing schedule than the meal schedule. In this situation, sandwiches will give you more time for fishing versus stopping for a shore lunch or returning to camp. It is not uncommon to be more than hour from camp when you start getting hungry.

However do not pass up the experience of a shore lunch. It is very much a part of the Canadian fishing trip. The natural surroundings and the taste of freshly caught fish add up to provide a truly enjoyable experience.

Allow yourself the flexibility of eating your meals around your fishing schedule. You can always eat; you may not always have a southwest wind. If the fish are biting you do not want to stop fishing. If plans are made to meet somewhere for lunch, you may want to have a mutual agreement that you will be there <u>unless</u> the fish are biting.

Water Travel _____

If you are fishing a large body of water for the first time you need to become familiar with landmarks on the lake. Visually familiarize yourself with portions of the lake you travel through. Occasionally look behind you so that you familiarize yourself with the way things will look on your return. Make mental notes such as "OK on my return I'll be going left of that island" or "It doesn't look like there is an outlet here, I'll have to remember this spot on my return, so I don't go past it." Keep in mind that shorelines will look different under different weather and light conditions. If necessary, orientate yourself using a compass and map. With a map and a compass you should be able to find your way around the lake or the portion of the lake you are fishing. Some bodies of water are so large that you may decide to fish only a portion of the lake. This is especially advisable if you find difficulty in orientating yourself. In these cases, you may decide to venture further as you become more familiar with leaving and returning to those areas closer to camp.

Depending on the size of the lake and your travel routes, after a few days you will become more familiar with your surroundings. On some very large lakes, marker buoys, lights or other manmade markers positioned on shore, assist you in navigating. Familiarize yourself with these locations. When you pass one, mentally record what direction you will go when returning to the marker.

Always watch for underwater obstructions. Just because you are in the middle of the lake does not mean that there are no underwater islands. A depth-finder with an alarm is very useful on new bodies of water. As soon as that alarm goes off, throttle back and watch for obstructions. If you are not using a depth-finder, position someone in the bow of the boat as a "spotter." Go slow enough so that you can quickly bring the boat to a stop when an obstruction is spotted.

If you are fishing any type of moving water you must be constantly alert to the dangers this water holds. Stay away from dams, the tops of rapids and waterfalls. Water is very dense and its force is very powerful. It can easily and quickly carry you into these areas.

If ocean fishing, be cognizant of tides and how they will affect your boating.

Lost or Stranded

Do not stay out late if you are far from camp. Always let the camp operator know the general area you will be fishing. A compass, map and knowledge of the direction you need to go, to get back to camp, is your best insurance against getting lost. If necessary, when traveling by water, follow your movement on the map.

If you would become lost or stranded, due to a damaged motor or motor failure, have an action plan in place. Be prepared. Your planning should include the possibility of camping overnight. In this case, you want to have insect repellant, a flashlight, matches, rain gear and at least a heavier shirt or jacket for warmth. The camp owner or someone in your fishing party will be out to pick you up in the morning. If it is a moonlit night, they may pick you up sooner.

There are several ways to assist your party in navigating. Marker buoys can be strategically placed on the lake especially at "forks." Markers can be placed in trees along shore. If some members of the fishing party stay out late, the first boat back to camp can set a lantern near the water to serve as a beacon for late arrivals. The types of warning lights that turn on at dark and flash, work well if all parties decide they want to stay out late.

CB radios, although not often used, offer another way of staying in touch with other members in your group. CB radios may require permits. Check with the Canadian information sources on acquiring permits for use of portable two-way radios.

Emergencies

Even though an emergency will probably not occur, you should know a distress signal which will be recognized as such. Ask your outfitter or camp owner what he would recommend doing if you have an emergency situation. Usually three of anything is recognized as a distress signal. Running tight circles in a boat is a signal. Internationally, a fluorescent orange cloth with black dot or square is recognized as a request for help. At an outpost a large bed sheet at the end of the dock should bring help. Some outposts have a flagpole which is used to signal for assistance.

Fish Cleaning, Cooking and Bears

If there are bears in the area DO NOT CLEAN FISH IN YOUR CABIN OR NEAR YOUR CAMP. Do not leave wet or smelly garbage in your cabin. Bears are attracted to anything with a strong smell. They are especially attracted to rotting garbage, fish guts and bacon grease. If you fry bacon, air out the cabin. Light up a cigar or burn some mosquito incense in the cabin prior to retiring for the night. If a dog is in camp make friends with the dog. Feed him some food and he will most likely sleep on your doorstep. He will start barking and growling when the bear comes around.

I will never forget the night my cousin and I had a large black bear scraping its claws on the small porch attached to our cabin. I went to look out the window next to the door and guess who was looking back at me about a foot away from the glass. It was Mr. Bear. My immediate vocal response apparently made him decide to visit someone else. He sauntered off into the dark, shaking his head (apparently at my reaction).

Clean your fish at a spot designated by the camp owner. In many areas fish entrails should not be thrown in the water. If the entrails are thrown in the water, the quantity of aquatic life may not be adequate enough to clean up the food before it begins to contaminate the water. If fish remains are left on shore and there are sea gulls in the area, they will clean up what you leave.

If camping, check with local authorities regarding bear precautions taken in the area. If bears are in the area, food should be tied in a tree a minimum of twelve feet from the ground and four feet from the trunk. The food and cooking area should be at least a hundred yards from the sleeping area. Do not take food into your tent and do not sleep in clothing permeated with the smell of food. Soap and toothpaste should be left with the food.

Other Activities

There are many things to do on a fishing trip besides fishing. Characteristically, the most sought after tourist attractions are part of the natural surroundings and Canada is rich in nature's creations.

The greens, blues and reds of the northern lights are spectacular and are intensified as you go further north. Wait for an evening when the sky is clear and get up after midnight for this captivating show.

Viewing wildlife can occupy many fascinating hours. Some of the larger land mammals you may see, depending on where you travel in Canada, can include deer, elk, moose, mountain lion and several species of bear. Closer to the arctic you can see musk-ox, caribou and polar bear. On the seacoasts, depending on the season, you may see whales, porpoises, sea otters, sea lions, walrus and seal.

Some of the smaller animals you may cross paths with will be beaver, otter, marten, lynx, coyote and possibly even a timber wolf. Always be watching because you will usually only get a glimpse of these wary creatures.

Among the birds you may see are eagles, loons, Canadian geese, ducks, osprey, herons, gulls and a multitude of songbirds. On the seacoast you will possibly see cormorants and puffins as well as many other seabirds.

Have your camera ready. Scenes abound for the photographer. Try some sunset or sunrise pictures near the water. Fog provides an interesting frame for pictures taken in the early morning. The different fauna and changing landscapes offer interesting and memorable shots.

Enjoy the quiet solitude. Swim or snorkel in the crystal clear lakes. Watch for a double rainbow or a very rare double-double rainbow. Pick blueberries. Go shopping. Visit the local historical sights. Also take opportunities to visit with other fishermen. Gather information for future trips. Visit with the owner or operator and with the local residents.

Chapter Nine

FISHING

Some areas will have so many hungry fish in them that any lure on any day in any weather will produce fish. Other areas will try your patience. The remainder of the spots will require a moderate amount of effort. Even in excellent waters there will be off days, days where the fish just will not hit anything. Weather, water conditions or abundance of food may at times contribute to this. This chapter discusses a majority of the Canadian game fish as well as topics which provide useful information for catching those fish.

The descriptions of the Canadian fish and how to catch them is not an in-depth scientific approach. The approach   taken is a more simplified one and provides you with information on lures, fishing methods and habitat that have produced fish in the past. Adapting this information to the waters you will be fishing will produce fish -- when the fish are biting!

Pre-Trip Planning _____

Well in advance of your trip, try to get a contour map of the lake you will be fishing. If river fishing, try to get a topographic map of the area. The resort owner or outfitter may have these maps. Also inquire of the Canadian information sources via their 800 phone numbers. Only a small percentage of Canadian lakes have contour maps. If a contour map of the lake does not exist, try obtaining a topographic map of the area. Study the map and decide which areas on the lake or river might have the right structure for the species you are after. Although it is difficult to guess what the lake bottom contours will be from looking at a topographic map, you will be able to see inlet streams and outlets, if they exist. This information can help you plan some fishing strategies as well as provide a navigational guide.

Always try to talk to someone that has fished the area before. They will be able to point out some good spots. If you are staying at a resort, the resort owner will also put you on some good spots. After all, he wants you to catch fish so that you will come back next season.

When you arrive in camp ask the other fishermen, already in camp, where to go. Most will be very helpful because generally there are popular spots that produce regularly and almost everyone openly shares this information. Also, use your intuition; no one in camp may know as much as you do about fishing.

When to Fish

Depending on the type of fishing trip you are on, your fishing times may have a set schedule. Other fishing trips may leave very open schedules. Ocean fishing may have a tighter time schedule especially if you are on a daily charter.

If no schedule has been set for your party, talk to the management, people that have fished the area before and other fishermen in camp about the best time to go out.

Your fishing schedule may depend on the species you are after. Walleyes, for example, like low light conditions. Northern and musky are sight feeders and like higher levels of light.

Let your schedule evolve. If you find you are fishing late and catching fish, then sleep later in the morning. You may decide that you want to be on the water at daybreak. If so, then you will most likely take a break during the day and fish in the evening or come off the water early in the day.

The weather, as well as the cooperation of the fish, will impact your daily fishing schedule.

The Fish

Some of the more popular species of fish angled for in Canada are described below. The descriptions of the fish are organized in sections which group together closely related fish. These sections will cover the trout, grayling, salmon, char, whitefish, perch, pike, mooneye, sturgeon and sunfish.

It is noteworthy to say that biological classifications include trout, salmon, char, whitefish and grayling in the *salmonid* family of fish. The grayling is often referred to as a trout. Although whitefish are not thought of as trout or salmon their value as table fare easily groups them with these fish.

The Atlantic salmon is more closely related to trout than it is to the Pacific salmon but is listed here under the salmons because of its common name.

Where fishing is dependent on spawning migrations only general references to spawning times are made. More specific times can be acquired by talking to your host, outfitter or the ministry in the area.

The Trout

Brown Trout: This favorite of fly fishermen, also called the German Brown, is a smart and wary fish. It is found in streams, rivers, the Great Lakes and the ocean. The migratory or sea-run brown trout is called a sea trout. The migratory brown is silvery with scattered black spots on the body. The sea-run brown resembles its cousin, the migratory rainbow trout or steelhead. A differentiating characteristic between the two are the spots covering the entire tail of the steelhead. Browns can be caught with flies, live bait, spinners and spoons. Their spawning runs occur in the fall.

<u>Rainbow Trout</u>: The rainbow trout can be caught with flies, live bait, spinners and spoons. Rainbows are fished for in lakes, rivers, the ocean and the Great Lakes. This fish is migratory but a landlocked cousin is called the kamloops trout.

The migratory rainbow is called a steelhead. The steelhead is considered a top-notch game fish and is often compared to the Atlantic salmon in fighting ability and acrobatics. When fishing steelhead, lures in red and orange colors are used with success. These lures imitate the color of salmon eggs, a favorite food of the steelhead. Fish plastic worms, spinners, spoons and plugs. Let the baits bounce along the bottom. These fish, unlike the salmon, will feed during their migrations. In rivers flowing to the ocean, main spawning runs occur in the winter and spring. Some runs will also occur at other times.

The steelhead closely resembles the chinook and coho salmon. To tell them apart, check the color of the mouth. The steelhead has a white mouth. The chinook and coho have black mouths.

<u>Cutthroat Trout</u>: The cutthroat exists in streams, rivers, lakes and may also migrate to the sea. The sea-run cutthroat are near the river mouths in the spring and summer. They will stay close to shore and are fished for from shore. In late summer they begin congregating at river mouths. Where found, they are fished for with fly, spinner and bait.

The Salmon

These fish are migratory, living in the ocean and spawning in freshwater. Salmon are fished for in both freshwater and saltwater. Provinces bordering the Great Lakes have salmon fishing where these species have been introduced to those waters. The Atlantic salmon exists on the East coast and five species of salmon exist on the West coast. The Pacific salmon are the chinook, coho, sockeye, pink and chum salmon.

Special gear is often used when fishing for these fighters. Rods are longer and have more flexible tips. Reels hold at least 300 yards of line.

Atlantic Salmon: The Atlantic salmon is another noted game fish due to its fight and acrobatics. It is a migratory fish and is more closely related to the trouts than to the Pacific salmons. The ouananiche (pronounced wa-na-neesh) is a landlocked freshwater form of the Atlantic salmon.

The Atlantic salmon does not die as a result of spawning as do the Pacific salmon. However many die after spawning due to bruises, infection and over-exertion. The survivors are called kelts or black salmon. After spawning, kelts return to the ocean taking as long as six months to make the journey.

Major spawning runs occur in the spring, summer and fall, although fish enter the rivers at all times of the year. The fish caught during the different seasons are referred to as "spring", "summer" and "autumn" salmon. The spring salmon is also called a "bright" salmon and is typically easier to catch than fish in later runs.

A grilse is a salmon that has been in the ocean for one year. For sizing and limit laws the ministry may classify a grilse as any fish under a certain size limit. Parr are young fish in the river which have not yet been in the ocean. A smolt is a parr that is migrating to the sea and has developed a silvery color.

Fishing for the Atlantic salmon in inland waters is generally restricted to fly fishing. In many areas it is required that larger salmon be released. Only the smaller grilse are kept. The ouananiche is caught trolling or spinning with silver colored wobblers and spoons and by fly casting.

When river fishing for salmon, ask what the average catch is. This varies depending on the area you are in and will alert you to a problem with your fishing methods.

<u>Chinook</u>: The chinook is often called the king salmon because it reaches the largest size among the Pacific salmons. It also goes by the name tyee and quinnat. Early runs of the chinook salmon produce fish referred to as "spring" salmon.

This fish will live in the ocean from three to five years before returning to freshwater to spawn. The spawning runs may occur from spring through fall but in some rivers only a fall run will be seen. Once hatched out, the fish will stay in freshwater from three months to four years before moving to the ocean.

In the ocean, trolling and mooching close to the bottom are methods used to catch these fish. In rivers, large wobbling spoons provide action by fishing them deep and slow. Spinners and flies are also used. Spinning and trolling are methods used in the Great Lakes.

Differentiating characteristics of the chinook are a black mouth and black gums.

<u>Coho</u>: Coho are also called silver salmon. The coho stays in the ocean for two to three years before migrating to freshwater to spawn in late fall. The fish enter rivers anywhere from June to October depending on the latitude. After hatch out, the fish will stay in freshwater for one to two years before turning silver and migrating to the ocean.

In rivers the coho will take bait, spinners, spoons and flies. Trolling and mooching are employed in ocean fishing. In the Great Lakes, spinning and trolling are typical fishing methods.

A distinguishing feature of the coho is its black mouth and white gums.

<u>Pink</u>: The pink salmon is also called the humpback salmon. Pink salmon runs are at higher levels on alternating years. In rivers, bright colored wet flies, spoons, spinners and wobblers, fished near bottom, produce fish. Casting to schools in river mouths is another popular method of fishing pinks.

<u>Sockeye</u>: The sockeye is also called the red salmon. In rivers, this fish is caught fishing wet flies near the bottom. A fly rod or light spinning gear is typical hardware.

<u>Chum</u>: Also called the dog salmon, these fish generally run later than the other salmons. These fish, although difficult to catch, will hit flies, spoons, spinners and wobblers.

The Char
Lake trout, brook trout, Arctic char and dolly varden all belong to a group of fish called char.

<u>Lake Trout</u>: Lake trout are also called grey trout, togue, mackinaw and lakers. Lake trout do not migrate but rather spawn in the lakes they inhabit. They prefer cold water. In the spring, lake trout can be found in shallow water. In the summer, as the surface water warms the trout will move to very deep levels. In bodies of water that stay cold all summer, typically lakes in the far north, the lakers will remain in shallow water all season.

When lake trout are shallow they will hit imitations of local forage fish. When deep, they can be fished for by either trolling, jigging a spoon or jigging bait. When jigging with a spoon, pull the spoon up and let it flutter back down. The trout will usually strike on the fall. Retrieve the lure quickly. If they missed the first strike they may hit the spoon again when it is moved quickly away from them. When the fish are deep they may be found in the evening or early morning in shallower water off deep water shorelines. Fish near the bottom when fishing for the laker.

The main distinguishing feature of the laker is a sharply forked tail. The sea-run brook trout will resemble a lake trout. The brook trout's tail will be more square than the tail of the laker.

<u>Brook Trout</u>: The brook trout has several other names; speckled trout, aurora trout and brookie. Brook trout found in the Great Lakes are sometimes called coasters. A cross between a brook trout and a brown trout is called a tiger trout. A wendigo or splake is a cross between a brook trout and a lake trout.

Sea-run brookies are called salters or sea trout. These trout change in appearance. They lose their color and become more silvery. In waters holding both Atlantic salmon and sea-run brook trout the brook trout can be distinguished from the salmon by its square tail, a long upper jaw line and a thicker body at the tail.

These fish can be caught with live bait and spinners. In streams and rivers, fish pools and deeper holes at the base of rapids. The nightcrawler is a popular live bait.

<u>Arctic Char</u>: This char is also called a blueback trout. In Quebec a close relative to the Arctic char is called the Quebec red trout. In the Arctic these fish migrate from freshwater to saltwater after the ice melts in May or June. They return anywhere between July and October and always prior to ice forming on the ocean waters.

These fish can be taken on large flies, spoons, spinners, plugs and jigs fished slowly and close to the bottom.

<u>Dolly Varden</u>: The dolly varden is also called a bull trout. It closely resembles the Arctic char. It likes moving water where oxygen levels are high. It is fished for with fly, spinners, bait and in deep lakes by trolling.

Grayling

This *salmonid* is caught on flies, small spoons and small spinners. Its habitat includes lakes, streams and rivers. Dark fly patterns are popular. A light fly rod or ultra-light spinning outfit is typically used.

The Whitefish

Several species of this member of the *salmonid* family exist in Canadian waters. Species are generally divided into two groups preferring either lakes or moving water. These two groups are represented by the lake whitefish and the mountain whitefish. Mountain whitefish and related species generally inhabit river and areas of moving water, not necessarily in the mountains. The lake whitefish and its related species are found in lakes. The inconnu or sheefish is a specie of whitefish.

In the lakes, whitefish can be found at all depths. In many lakes, whitefish as well as ciscoe are forage fish for larger sized game fish. These fish can often be found suspended over deep water.

Whitefish feed on insects and can be caught with a fly rod. Whitefish can be caught using bait, a small spinner or a small spoon. The mouth of a whitefish is very small and tender and as a result small tackle and gentle play is necessary when fishing them.

The Pike

Northern Pike: This fish is nick-named the jack or jackfish. Northerns like weeds and structure close to deeper water. Northerns will also suspend when the water becomes warm close to shore. Northerns are very aggressive when they are hungry and will hit any lure within sight. The larger northern tend to feed like their cousin the muskie. They will feed, fill up and then digest their food over several days. During this digesting period they will not strike at anything. Spinners and spoons are good northern lures. Larger spinners are also effective.

Muskellunge: The muskie is a true trophy because of the patience it takes to catch one, its wariness and its size. Bucktail spinners are top producers. Jerk baits and diving plugs are also popular lures. Suckers are also used during different parts of the year. Trolling, where permitted, is as effective as casting. Muskies like weeds and camouflaging structure from which they can launch a sudden short-distanced attack. A cross between a northern pike and a muskellunge is called a tiger muskie.

Chain Pickerel: This smaller cousin of the muskie and northern is found in habitat similar to that preferred by those fish. Bait, spinners, spoons and plugs are used to catch this little fighter.

The Perch

Walleye: Also named walleyed pike, yellow walleye and pickerel, the walleye likes moving water, even if it is only a slight current. In the spring of the year, walleye will congregate where there is a faster flow of water. Towards summer the walleye will tend to disburse throughout a lake with some fish remaining near faster water.

Walleyes prefer feeding under low light conditions. On bright days, action tends to be better in the morning and evenings. On overcast days fishing will typically be better than on bright clear days.

Fish shorelines that the wind is blowing to. Fish jigs tipped with natural bait, crankbait lures or spinners close to the bottom. If walleyes are suspended, troll a fast action minnow type lure or still-fish with a slip-bobber rig.

Jigging is overall the most productive method for catching walleye. Once you learn the method it will produce for you. It is not complicated and it is one of the most productive methods for fishing walleye. Jigging is simply raising and lowering a jig. When lowering the jig keep the line taut. Use the lightest possible jig to maintain a vertical presentation. Walleye typically hit the jig when it is being lowered. The hit may be very light or there may be no hit at all; the line will just not continue to fall. Set the hook at the slightest irregularity. In doing this, you should set the hook on anything that feels or looks different. You will often set the hook when the jig bumps a rock or a snag but this is necessary in catching the light hitters. Popular jig colors are white, yellow and pink. Minnows, leeches and nightcrawlers are popular bait.

A sensitive rod is important when jigging for walleyes. You have to be able to feel the jig and any change in its weight or movement. When choosing a rod for its sensitivity, hold the rod and ask someone to gently tap the end of the rod. You want to be able to feel a very slight tap.

Sauger: The sauger is a very close relative of the walleye and many times is mistaken for a walleye. Also named the sand pickerel or sand pike this fish likes the same type of habitat that the walleye prefers. Fishing techniques used for the walleye can also be used for the sauger.

Yellow Perch: This panfish likes weeds and any structure that offers protection against predators. Generally live bait is used to catch this tasty fish. Worms are a popular live bait.

The Sunfish

The Canadian sunfish include the smallmouth bass, largemouth bass, black crappie, white crappie, bluegill, pumpkinseed, redbreast sunfish, longear sunfish and rock bass. Except for the smallmouth and largemouth bass, the sunfish fall into the commonly referred to group of fish called panfish. These fish prefer live bait although they will hit artificials. Crappies readily take small live minnows. The bluegills and sunfish like worms and insect larva. The sunfish prefer weeds and brush or any type of structure that offers some cover.

Smallmouth Bass: Smallmouths like rocks, weeds, brush and underwater reefs. They prefer gravel or rock bottoms. Popular lures are minnow and grayfish imitating crankbaits.

Largemouth Bass: Largemouth bass are generally not choosy when it comes to a meal. Slowly retrieved worm-like lures produce well. Since the larger bass feed mainly on other fish, minnow imitating lures also produce well. For structure, the largemouth like weeds, brush, stumps and logs.

The Mooneyes

Mooneye: The mooneye inhabits larger lakes and streams. It prefers clearer water than its cousin the goldeye. Lures and live bait are used to catch the mooneye. Its eyes are large and silvery in color.

Goldeye: The goldeye inhabits silty water in larger lakes and rivers. Like the mooneye, lures and live bait are both used in catching the goldeye. Its eyes are large and golden in color.

The Sturgeon

Lake, white, green and Atlantic sturgeon are among the different species of sturgeon found in Canada. The white, green and Atlantic sturgeon are closely related. These sturgeon are bottom feeders but will also feed on fish. The lake sturgeon is a bottom feeder. Worms or nightcrawlers are a favorite bait when fishing for sturgeon.

Shad

This relative of the herring is fished for when it migrates from the ocean and enters rivers in spring and summer. Small bright jigs, flies, small spinners and spoons are used to catch this fish.

Ocean Fish

When ocean fishing for the sea-run trouts and the salmons you may also want to pursue some of the many ocean fishes.

On the Pacific coast, some of the favorite species sought are halibut, red snapper, ocean perch, flounder, cod and lingcod. Cut herring is a favorite bait. It is bottom fished, trolled and "mooched." Mooching is drift fishing.

On the Atlantic coast, tuna, striped bass, bluefish, cod, pollock and mackerel are some of the more often fished for species. Tuna require special gear. Lures are used for bluefish. Striped bass are fished in a variety of ways. Cod and mackerel are jigged. Bait or brightly feathered jigs are used for pollock.

Distinguishing Features _____

Fish similar in appearance inhabiting the same waters are sometimes difficult to identify. The following condensed reference may be helpful if you run into the problem.

Walleye --
> Dark area at rear of dorsal fin between last 2-3 spines.

Sauger --
> No dark area at rear of dorsal fin, spotted dorsal fin and dark saddle-like bands on sides of fish.

Muskellunge --
> 6-9 sensory pores on each side of lower jaw.

Tiger muskie --
> distinct vertical silvery bars on sides of fish.

Northern pike --
> 5 sensory pores on each side of lower jaw.

Chain pickerel --
> chain-like body markings.

Steelhead	-- white mouth.
Chinook	-- black mouth -- black gums.
Coho	-- black mouth -- white gums.

| Brook trout | -- square tail. |
| Lake trout | -- forked tail. |

Sea-run brook trout --
> square tail, mouth extends past eye, usually 9 rays in anal fin, light body spots.

Sea-run dolly varden --
> squarish tail, mouth extends past eye, light body spots, no markings on tail or dorsal fins.

Sea-run cutthroat --
> squarish tail, small dark spots over entire fish.

Sea-run brown trout --
> squarish tail, anal fin has ten or less rays, mouth extends past the eye, dark body spots.

Steelhead --
> squarish tail, 10 or less rays in anal fin, jaw extends to or just pass the eye, dark body spots.

Atlantic salmon --
> tail is not square, jaw line does not extend past eye, dark body spots.

Pacific salmon --
> longer anal fin, 13-19 rays.

Dolly varden --
 Spots usually smaller than the diameter of the fishes eye.
Arctic char --
 Spots usually larger than the diameter of the fishes eye.

Smallmouth bass -- mouth extends to eye.
Largemouth bass -- mouth extends past center of eye.
Rock bass   -- red in eye.

Fishing Tips

A lure is most effective when it imitates the natural food available to the fish. A lure with excessive vibration imitates a wounded or fleeing fish. A spinner sends out vibrations which attracts a fish.

Combining wire leaders with some types of lures may impede their action. With these lures use a loop knot that does not close when tightened.

The color of the lure has some impact on your success. Fluorescent colors retain their original color at greater depths than non-fluorescent colors. Fluorescent colored lures may produce more fish in colored water. As a general rule use lighter colored lures on bright days and darker lures on darker days.

When trolling several lines, all lines must have lures that function optimally at the set trolling speed. Fishing partners using the same boat should discuss this before the trip so that both parties take equivalent lures for trolling.

Look for structure. Structure includes weeds, bars, reefs, drop-offs, saddles, points and a change in bottom material. Find the structure that is holding the food and you will find the fish. Once identified, that structure may also produce for you in other parts of the lake. It also may not. Some fishermen believe that 90% of the fish are in 10% of the lake. If this is true then you have to find that 10%. If you know what the fish are hitting on and they are not biting where you are fishing, do not spend more than 15 minutes in that spot.

Fish have a sense of smell. Some scents will alarm a fish. Human scent is at the top of this list. The smell of a predator fish will also alarm another fish. If you catch a northern while fishing for walleye, thoroughly wash your hands and your lure of the northern smell. A fish when caught will give off a smell which warns other fish of its species that there is danger. Because of this you may want to avoid getting the slime of the fish on the lure you are using.

Be quiet and do not wear bright clothing. Big fish got that way because they recognize something different in their environment and reacted with more caution.

When fishing new territory ask someone familiar with the area what size of fish are caught on average in that area. Your first fish may be a trophy and you might want to consider taking some pictures before you release or fillet it.

If you are going after larger fish, heavier two-handed "long-butt" rods are recommended. These rods provide leverage when casting, retrieving and setting the hook. The added leverage can make the job of casting large lures much less tiring. A rod with a long butt is easier to hold with one hand especially when trolling and running the motor at the same time. In this situation the butt can be positioned under the forearm for greater leverage. These rods should contain larger reels with between 20 and 35 lb. test line. If you plan on doing a lot of casting, you will most likely prefer to keep your line on the lighter side of this range. If you are after big northern or musky in an area with a lot of weeds then you need the strength of a heavier line to prevent the line from breaking when those fish start "mowing" the weeds.

When fly fishing for large game fish use a large reel with at least 220 yards of backing.

For trolling and casting smaller lures for smaller fish, a medium rod and reel combination is needed.

For jigging, a one piece rod usually provides more sensitivity. I like the rods that go all the way through the handle. Some materials used in the construction of rods are advertised as being more sensitive than others. Reels are primarily a personal choice. I personally like an open face reel on my jigging rod because the rod and reel remain in one hand at all times; in my case the right hand because I am right handed. Because I am right-handed, my coordination with this hand and arm are better for feeling hits and reacting more quickly.

Rod, Reel & Line Maintenance

Periodically during the day, after a snag and after fighting a big fish, check the last 4-5 feet of your line for abrasions. Do this by sliding the line between your thumb and index finger. If you feel any abrasions, cut off the line and re-tie your knots. You may also want to periodically retie your knots.

Also, periodically check your drag. Most large fish are lost because of an improperly set drag. The drag should be tight enough to enable you to make a good hook set and also let the fish pull some line off the reel if he makes a run. The drag should not be so tight that the line breaks. If a fish, especially a large fish, cannot take line, he may pull the hooks right out of his mouth. However, if you plan on releasing a large fish you want to get the fish to the boat or shore quickly rather than playing him for a long time. The longer the fish is under exertion the poorer his chances for survival after release.

Prior to your trip, tighten all reel screws. Periodically, during the trip, visually check reels for loose hardware and check your guides for abrasions.

Twists may develop in your fishing line. These twists can be the result of playing a fish, using a faulty lure or putting new line on a spool. Snarls that develop are usually a result of this twisted line. To prevent snarls in your line and to eliminate the twist in the line, remove all hardware and play the twisted line out behind the boat while the boat is moving. In a short period of time the friction of the water against the line will untwist the line. Reel it in and tie on your snap, leader or lure.

If a lot of line has been removed from your open face reel, the friction of the line against the spool will affect your casting accuracy. Knowing this will allow you to adjust your cast accordingly. Loss of line from the spool will also increase the drag which, if not adjusted, could cost you a fish. When re-filling your spool fill the spool until the line is just below the edge of the spool. When re-filling a spool try to wind the line onto the spool in the same direction or circle that it comes off the store spool. This will help eliminate twists in the line.

If you are using any reels that contain bail springs, you may want to buy an extra bail spring for the reel and put it in your tackle box. These springs rarely break but if one breaks on your favorite reel, while fishing in some remote area, you will appreciate having the spare.

Fishing Knots

Using the proper knot is important. A proper fishing knot can prevent the loss of a fish. Many knots exist for tying your line to snaps, leaders, another line or directly to the lure. Knots recommended by fishing line manufacturers are good knots. Directions for tying these knots are usually included with the line.

Prior to your trip, experiment with the knots you will use to fasten lines to leaders, lures or snaps. Some knots, when tightened, will actually squeeze the line and make the diameter of the line smaller until it parts. You want to use a knot that does not do this. To test a knot, take a piece of fishing line and tie each end of the line to a snap. Using two pair of pliers, grab a snap with each pliers and pull until the line breaks. If the line continuously breaks at the knot, the knot is most likely the cause. Try a different knot.

Get a good knot book and practice tying those knots you want to use in your type of fishing.

Boating & Camping Knots

Proper camping and boating knots can prevent loss of time and can also prevent accidents. There are several knots that have traditionally been used more often than other knots for boating and camping; these are the square knot, the half hitch and the bowline. Another favorite of mine is the clove hitch.

Clove Hitch

This simple knot can be tied quickly and easily especially when it is being fastened to a piling or any object it can be slipped over. With the rope in front of you and with the end of the rope pointing to your left, grasp the rope about two feet from the end with your left hand turned upward. Then grasp the rope with your right hand facing downward. Put two loops in the rope by turning both hands clockwise. Place the loop held in your right hand over the loop held in your left hand and slide both loops over the piling. Secure this clove hitch by adding a half-hitch.

 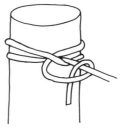

Half Hitch

This knot has a variety of uses. It is used for lashing things down. It can be used in camping where a line needs to adjusted periodically. It is easy to untie because much of the pressure of the line is exerted on the first hitch. Succeeding hitches take less and less of the pressure.

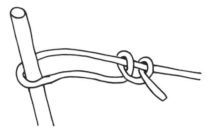

Bowline

This knot is primarily used to put a loop in the end of a rope. The loop will not close as pressure is applied to it.

Square Knot

This knot is used for lashing things down.

Safety _____

Life jackets and/or life cushions must be accessible at all times. If you feel you need to wear one then do so. Do not second guess your intuition in matters of safety. If you decide not to wear one then have one near you. In cold weather, when the water is cold, and when you are wearing a lot of clothing you will need a flotation device to stay afloat. If you are fishing in a situation that might cause you to fall from the boat, wear a life jacket.

Fast moving water is perilous, especially above a rapids or waterfall. It demands the utmost respect and caution. Tides may also pose hazards that require taking precautions. Books and schedules are available which list the timing of the tides

If winds pick up and you have difficulty controlling your craft due to waves, point your boat into the waves. Do this even if it means taking a less direct route back to your camp. If this is not possible, find a place protected from the wind and wait for the wind to subside.

If you are unsure of what boating safety entails, take a safety course and read a book on water safety.

Catch and Release _____

Catch and release policies are here to stay. In trophy areas it is many times either the law or a policy of the resort. In the far north it may take 50+ years to produce a 30 pound trout. Because of this it is wise to avoid destroying these fish indiscriminately.

In playing and releasing a fish, stress to the fish can be minimized by quickly getting the fish to the boat. Some people believe there is a point of no return if the fish fights too long. Since they will fight until they die, after a long fight they may be near that point and will not be able to recover.

If possible, measure large fish while keeping the fish in the water. Do not pick these fish up and hold them vertically. This may harm them. Also, try not to remove any of the slime from the skin of the fish. This slime protects the fish from many diseases. In general, try to handle the fish as little as possible. It will have a better chance for survival.

Chapter Ten

WEATHER & FISHING

You know where you will fish, the lures and bait you will use, but what about the weather? The weather will equally influence your fishing methods and fishing success. It is helpful to know what weather signs mean and to use them in predicting what weather is headed your way. Knowing how the weather may change or being able to predict, to some degree, how long the current weather will remain will help you plan your fishing for the day.

For safety reasons, when you are fishing an area where unanticipated weather may pose a safety hazard, ask someone familiar with the area to tell you the weather signs to watch for.

The Barometer, Wind Direction and Weather Prediction

With very little effort you can generally forecast the weather using a barometer and observing the changing direction of the wind. When the wind changes, typically the weather will begin to change. The winds of a low pressure system will tend to move in a counter-clockwise direction. High pressure systems have winds moving generally in a clockwise direction. By using a barometer to substantiate the low or high pressure moving towards you, you can better predict what weather is headed your way.

The barometer indicates air pressure which indicates the weight of the air. Heavier air will cause a barometer to have a higher reading. This is referred to as a "high." Higher air pressure prevents moisture in the air from condensing and as a result high pressure systems are usually associated with clearer weather. When air pressure drops any water in the air will have a tendency to condense. This condensation results in clouds and rain. This drop in atmospheric pressure is referred to as a "low."

The difference in pressure between two locations will cause air to move from the high pressure area to the low pressure area. Wind strength is dependent on how fast pressure differences occur and the difference in pressure between two weather systems. The faster the barometer moves, the faster the weather will change.

The chart on the following page summarizes typical weather when the barometer is moving from different pressure levels and the wind has changed from one direction to another.

Weather's Effect on Fishing

To different degrees, weather affects fish and their feeding habits. Fish tend to feed more voraciously during specific weather conditions. Certain types of weather will have a negative effect on fishing and some weather provides for fair fishing.

I have found that good fishing is usually associated with a rapidly falling barometer which also indicates an approaching storm. I watch for a wind shift from the west to a southwest direction. This is a counterclockwise shift, and with a drop in barometer, it signals an approaching storm. This change in wind and barometric pressure will bring on good fishing. Because fish apparently do not like extended periods of low pressure, they tend to feed heavily prior to the storm. Their feeding then drops off as the low settles in. These extended lows are sometimes referred to as "cold fronts."

Fishing will usually remain poor until the barometer again changes. If the low pressure remains steady for more than two days, fishing should improve. During periods of low pressure, fish smaller lures and baits while using slower retrieves.

Barometer Movement	Wind Shift	Weather Forecast
High & Falling	S to SE	Rain in 24 hrs
	SE or E to NE	Rain in 12 hrs
Mid Range & Falling	SE to NE	Rain for 12-48 hrs
Falling	W to S	Storm
Low & Falling	S to E	Severe Storm
Rising	Clockwise to West	Clearing

Barometer & Wind

Weather Forecaster

Rainy days, associated with low pressure systems, do not adversely affect fishing. DO NOT fish in the rain if that rain is part of a thunderstorm. The thunderstorm will usually pass with the front that brought the weather in.

As the barometer begins to rise, fishing will improve and generally remains consistent until the barometer again begins to fall.

When fishing, watch the wind. Wind will drive plankton to shore. This attracts the rest of the food chain all the way up to the game fish. If the wind is very strong and your craft is built for rough water, you might want to try using a sea-anchor and drift fish on these very windy days.

Many of the correlations you make between weather and fishing success are the result of your experience. You learn these from many hours of fishing. For this reason you may find it helpful to keep a log of weather patterns and fishing successes; yours and others. After doing this for some time, you will see patterns develop in your data.

Some fishing success is the result of being at the right location for the current weather pattern. If you know a storm is approaching you may have a favorite spot that has produced fish for you just prior to a storm. Or you may have a favorite spot during bright sunny days. Or you may have found that wind blowing against a certain shore will produce fish in that area.

Weather Signs

Many things in nature can be signs of impending weather changes. Animals, cloud formations, rainbows, thunder, sunsets and the night sky are some of the things you can observe. All these things can assist you in making your forecast.

Clouds are one of the more obvious indicators. Any cloud in the sky is the result of the accumulation of moisture. If the clouds are low and moving in your direction you might get rain. Generally the lower the clouds are, the more they are associated with poor weather. Very low clouds which seem to "hang in the trees" usually predict the bad weather will stick around for a longer period of time. Thunderheads, those clouds extending from the ground up to many thousands of feet, are formed by a clash of two weather systems. Thunderstorms and lightning will accompany these clouds.

Weather systems travel generally in a westerly to easterly direction. The winds in these weather systems would be coming from the southwest, northwest, or west. If you see a rainbow in the west, it is likely that the rain that helped create the rainbow is moving in an easterly direction and that you might be in its path. If dark black clouds are west of you, be prepared to take cover or head for camp. There is a good chance the weather associated with those clouds is moving towards you. Sunsets can also indicate what clouds and moisture exist west of you.

The activities of animals many times tell you things about the weather. When birds feed during a rain, it usually indicates the rain will last for some time.

Observe the night sky. A clear night sky indicates the presence of a high pressure system. A halo around the moon indicates moisture in the air.

Seasonal Weather Patterns_____

The spring and fall turnover in the lakes, if it occurs at all, can affect fishing. Turnover occurs when surface waters at a different temperature than underlying waters are pushed to one side of the lake by wind and are then mixed with the underlying waters. Fall turnover disorientates the fish and can throw the fishing off for a few days. Spring turnover can have an effect but is not usually a noticeable factor affecting the fishing.

Weather which causes early or late seasonal changes can dramatically affect a fishing trip. If a party has, for years, fished only during the spring and then one year the winter is very mild which in turn causes a very early spring, this party may find themselves fishing in the summer period even though the calendar says it is supposed to be spring. In these cases, and depending on the locale, the fishing may be slower and fishing techniques may have to be adjusted.

Chapter Eleven

FILLETING & PACKAGING

Keeping your fish well preserved and getting them home in that state is important to the successful conclusion of a good trip.

The different provinces and territories may have different laws on the wrapping or packaging of fish for purposes of examining and counting one's catch. Fish may need to be individually wrapped in clear plastic packaging. Skin or a portion of the skin may need to be left attached to fillets. With length and slot sizes becoming more and more common, packaging requirements may also become more strict. Check with the government information sources for the province or territory you will fish regarding any packaging restrictions.

Filleting Fish

For cleaning fish, a good quality knife is a must. The majority of fishermen use a fillet knife for cleaning their fish. These fillet knives come in different lengths. Many people use the knife they have become accustomed to over the years. For the beginner, a decision needs to be made on how they would like to fillet their fish and then choose the appropriate knife.

There are two general methods of filleting fish. These methods are detailed below. Method #1 cuts the ribs away from the backbone and later the ribs are removed from the fillet. Method #2 removes the fillet while leaving the ribs attached to the backbone.

The first method requires more pressure in separating the ribs from the backbone. The knife is usually longer than the fish is wide. A shorter fillet knife and even a jackknife will work when using the second method.

Either method is quite easy after it is practiced a short time. To eliminate frustration and a poor fillet job, keep your knife very sharp and check it daily to see if it has lost its edge. There are many sharpening devices on the market today and many of these are compact units. Personally, I prefer a small three inch sharpening stone which I keep right in my tackle box.

Although it is more work, many fishermen like the skin left on the fillets of some species. Some species, notably the trouts and salmons, very seldom have their skins removed. If you want to leave the skin on the heavier scaled fish, scale the fish before you dress or fillet them.

On some species of fish, notably walleye, the "cheeks" can be removed from the head of the fish.

Filleting Method #1

Lay the fish on a flat surface with the back of the fish facing you. Take the fillet knife and cut downward behind the fins on the side of and near the head of the fish. When the knife reaches the back bone, slide the knife along the backbone towards the tail. With this cut you will separate the ribs from the backbone. Near the tail, cut through the backbone and flip the fish over. Slide the knife forward along the backbone until you reach the head. At this point cut through the skin. You will now have two fillets connected at the tail. Before skinning the fillets use the tip of the fillet knife and fillet out the rib bones connected to the fillets. Skin the fillet by grasping the tail and with the skin side down slide your fillet knife along the skin separating the skin from the flesh. Do this for the other fillet.

If you want an even fancier "butterfly" fillet, do not separate the fillets at the stomach of the fish. Your two fillets will be connected at this point and when laid flat will be shaped somewhat like a butterfly.

Filleting Method #2

On both sides of the fish make a cut at the back of the head downward along the side of the fish. Do not cut too deep. Try to cut only the meat. Then open the stomach by cutting forward from the vent to the cuts previously made. Also make a cut on each side of the anal fin from the vent to the tail. With the back of the fish towards you, make a cut along the backbone from the head to the tail as in method #1. Do not cut through the ribs. Instead slide the tip of the fillet knife down to the point where the ribs attach to the backbone and then, using several strokes of the knife, gently slide the knife along the ribs and cut the fillet from the ribs. When the ribs are free finish cutting along the backbone towards the tail. Then skin the fillet as noted in method #1.

If freezer space allows, gutting and removing the gills from your fish is an option to filleting your fish in camp. I prefer this method because it allows me more time to more carefully fillet my fish at home. If you do this, ensure that all gill membranes are cut from the fish and that the body cavity is well cleaned, the air bladder is removed and the kidney, the red bloody tissue along the backbone, is removed.

Preservation

Your preservation techniques are dependent upon what equipment is available to you at your camp. The less remote locations will have freezers running on electricity. Propane refrigerators and freezers are common in remote areas. If an electric generator is available, some refrigeration and freezer units might be connected to it.

At some locations, the refrigeration and freezer space may be confined. Ask the camp operator what facilities are available prior to your trip and preferably before you sign-up.

If you are at an outpost the owner may occasionally fly in ice and also fly out any trophies.

In salmon fishing areas, canning or smoking facilities may be available to you. Or you may want to can your salmon right at your camp site.

Packaging and Packing _____

Clear air-tight plastic bags are a good choice for packaging fillets or whole fish. For whole fish, I use bread bags saved during the year. Masking tape works well for taping the bags shut. A waterproof marking pen is needed to label the package with the specie name and the owner's name. This is very important for keeping track of limits.

Keep a score-card or make log entries as to number of fish put in the freezer and by whom. This will prove invaluable when you start scratching your head, wondering how many more fish you can keep before you are over limit. Towards the end of the trip verify your tally sheet against what you have cached in the freezer. Being just one over the limit is not worth the associated fine and confiscation of all your fish. So make sure your counts are accurate.

Preserving Trophies   _____

If you catch a fish which you want mounted and you are unskilled at skinning and preserving hides, you will need to take your trophy home whole. Because of dehydration which causes shrinkage, as soon as you have the fish out of the water and definitely before you put the fish in the freezer, measure and weigh the fish. Measure length and girth. The girth should be taken at several points. Make a rough drawing of the fish and indicate on the drawing what the measurements were at the different points. This information will be invaluable to your taxidermist.

There are various opinions on how to best preserve your fish until you can get it to your taxidermist. Generally, the fins scales and skin of the fish should not be allowed to dry out. If the fish can be frozen, keep the fish from drying out by wrapping it in plastic. Always protect the fins with cardboard and if possible wrap the fish in something rigid. Cardboard will work for this also. Tape with masking tape and freeze the fish as soon as possible.

If refrigeration is not available, I am told that borax can be used to preserve the fish. This preservation method suggests rubbing borax over the entire fish and then letting it air dry for about two hours in a shady area. If the fish cannot be frozen immediately after this, it should be gutted and gilled and borax should also be applied to the inside of the fish. The fins should be positioned with cardboard prior to drying.

Chapter Twelve

COOKING THE CATCH

Unless you are a chef and enjoy a lot of preparation you will most likely appreciate recipes that are not time consuming and still result in a delicious meal. This chapter provides some tips on planning meals as well as some simple and delicious recipes for cooking fish.

Meal Planning

If you are camping or housekeeping at a resort, try to plan your meals prior to your trip. You will want to consider the number of people in your party, their appetites, their likes and dislikes, ease of packing the ingredients, weight and cost of foods. Do not plan on eating only fish on your trip. Most fishing parties will generally eat fish once a day. This means you need to consider what you will eat at the other meals and what you will eat with the fish. You may also want to consider taking freeze dried foods and dehydrated beverages especially if you are camping or taking a river trip.

Camp life is a lot easier if your meals are planned as much as possible in advance of your trip. Once in camp, your other activities will most likely dictate when you will eat. The "when" will sometimes dictate "what" you will eat. For example, you do not want to prepare an elaborate meal after fishing until midnight. In this case your party will probably be very happy with sandwiches. This means no dishes, very little cleanup, everyone generally preparing their own food and no delay in getting to bed. Who wants to do dishes at midnight?

Plan some "rainy day" meals for those days where you might be in camp for a longer portion of the day. This might be the day for a meal that takes a little more time or is more involved.

Unless you want your schedule to be dictated by meal preparations, it is advisable to plan meals that are easy to prepare. Sandwiches fill a need and you may want to consider this option in certain cases. Meals prepared at home, frozen and then reheated are an option if you can keep these dishes frozen long enough. If you do not know how long your coolers will keep food frozen, either experiment or write to the manufacturer.

Shore Lunches

Fish cooked soon after they are caught have an exceptional taste. If you are on a trip that offers the opportunity to have a shore lunch, by all means have one. If you have one, you will most likely schedule several. The shore lunch, where practical, is very much a part of any fishing trip. The taste of the fish is definitely one of the reasons for the existence of this fishing tradition. This and the "atmosphere" of the Canadian outdoors makes this a truly memorable experience.

Shore lunch preparation can be simple. The cooking time can be quick. Potatoes, beans or just plain bread are simple but tasty compliments to the fish.

Any of the recipes below can be used for a shore lunch. If American fries are on the menu, cook these potatoes the evening or morning before. This will save you a lot of time and give you more time to fish.

When cooking with frying pans over a wood fire use a grate if possible. The grate should be nine to ten inches above the base of the fire. Start your fire and let it burn down. Begin cooking and feed the fire as necessary to maintain adequate temperature. Locate a flat rock near your fire to be used to set the pan on in case the fire gets too hot.

When you are finished cooking, insure the fire is put out. Pour enough water into the fire pit so that the ashes are underwater. Stir up the ashes to insure that water permeates the entire pit.

If you do not have a grate and do not want to pack frying pans, a folding wire grill which holds your food between two grills is another way of grilling. The grill is turned to cook both sides of the fish. Fish spitted on a green piece of branch is yet another way of cooking this delicious fare.

An alternative to wood fires is a camp stove. Using a camping stove will typically speed up your shore lunch, allowing more time for fishing. The disadvantage in using a stove is the packing of another piece of gear.

Recipes for Fish _____

There are hundreds of ways of preparing fish. Some of these methods are quite complicated. The recipes which follow are not. If a recipe is simple and the result tasty, what more can you ask for?

Quantity of fish is not mentioned in some of these recipes because that is determined just prior to meal time. Each person will have to tell the cook how much they can eat. If the cook has done this before he or she will probably have a good idea of how much to make and will not have to ask.

Spices and staples you might want to consider taking are salt, pepper, garlic powder, lemon juice, brown and white sugar.

Recipe #1   Quick Shore Lunch
This simple recipe calls for only three ingredients; fish, butter and salt. Over moderate heat (I have already set a cast iron pan directly on top of burning charcoal) melt enough butter to coat the fry pan. Add fillets and saute'. Turn fish as necessary. Fish are cooked when the meat flakes. Remove from pan and salt to taste. Small red potatoes, boiled, cut up and warmed in a frying pan are a nice compliment to the fish.

Recipe #2   Traditional Shore Lunch

Take one or more paper bags depending on number of people eating. Partially fill each bag with either flour, cornmeal or cracker crumbs. Add salt and pepper (do not add salt if you are using salted cracker crumbs). Dip the fillets in egg batter. Bread fillets by dropping one or two fillets at a time into the bag of breading. Shake the bag and remove the coated fillets. When all fillets are breaded, deep fry them in a large frying pan filled with lard heated to a high temperature. Vegetables served at shore lunches are typically beans, potatoes or both. Potatoes can be french-fried (takes more oil and heat) or raw-fried (takes more time) or American-fried (fast, if pre-cooked).

Recipe #3   Uncle Seabass' Breaded Fish

Coat fillets with egg and cracker crumbs by dipping them in a beaten egg mixture and then turning them in cracker crumbs. Fry in butter over moderate heat. Small red potatoes served as American-fries are a nice compliment to the fish. Another vegetable and a small steak can also be added to enhance this meal.

Recipe #4   Dad's Favorite Baked Fish

Place fish and several thin slices of onion in heavy foil. Salt and pepper. Sprinkle with a few drops of lemon juice. Enclose the fish totally by folding the foil twice at the edges. Place over moderate heat and bake until done. Baking time will vary depending on your heat source. A good heavy bread is a nice compliment to the baked fish.

Recipe #5   Sean's Fish Boil

Any fish with a higher oil content is suitable for this poaching technique. Cut fish into wide "steak" portions. Add salt and several drops of lemon juice to a kettle of cold water. Place the fish in the kettle of water before heating the water (do not preheat the water). Bring water to a simmer and cook until done.

Recipe #6   Allanwater Fish Chowder
 Ingredients:
    2 cans (10 3/4 oz) Cream of Potato soup
    2 cans (10 3/4 oz.) Cream of Celery soup
    1 small (6-8 oz.) can of mixed vegetables
    12 oz. (approx.) canned condensed milk
    1/3 cup coarsely chopped red onion
    1 large green pepper, coarsely chopped
    2/3 lb. heavy smoked bacon
    1 to 1-1/2 lb. of fillets, cut into 1" pieces
    Salt and pepper

Cut bacon into pieces and saute'. When bacon grease covers bottom of pan, add onion and green pepper and saute'. Drain off any bacon grease. Add vegetables with liquid, soup and two cans of water. Simmer. Add salt and pepper to taste. Add raw fish and simmer for 5 minutes. Add evaporated milk just before serving. Do not allow the soup to boil after the milk is added. Serve with a heavy crusted bread and butter. Serves four.

Cooking Tips

Try cooking fish and meats over a hardwood fire using a grate or a hinged basket grill. A wood fire gives the food an excellent smoky flavor. For added smoke flavor, throw into the fire some hickory, alder or apple wood chips pre-soaked in water. This will "spice" up your meal. Smoked fish are delicious.

For fish and meats, the basket grill is very useful. This grill can be rotated thus exposing both sides of the fish or meat to the fire. For cooking over wood fires with frying pans, a light-weight grate proves very helpful.

Fish longer than twelve to fourteen inches should be cut into fillets rather than cooked whole.

Desserts in camp are usually different than at home because of the packing involved. Bread, butter and jelly seems common when at home but in camp it becomes a very delicious treat. Canned fruit, such as canned raspberries, is another easily packed dessert.

For between meal snacks, prior to the trip, mix up some dried foods and put portions in sealable plastic bags. Popcorn is a real treat around camp.

The potatoes for American-fries can be boiled the night before or in the early morning prior to going out. They will then only need to be cut and heated at lunch.

Example Food List _____

This list contains food items taken by four adults on a six day fishing trip. Each person brought their own snacks and beverages. This list corresponds to a number of recipes mentioned above. The list is a starting point. Modify it to fit your needs. These rations were supplemented with fish at one meal each day. All meats were frozen with the exception of the chicken which was eaten on day one. The butter was also frozen. Frozen food was packed with two, one gallon jugs of frozen water in a twenty quart cooler. Freezer facilities existed at the lodge and some items were placed in the freezer and kept frozen there until they were ready to use.

Whenever possible try to buy items packaged in plastic containers versus glass.

___ 8 beef fillets (approx. 4 lbs.)
___ 3 lbs. of ground beef (made 8 burgers)
___ 2 roasted chickens

__ 10 bratwurst sausages
__ 4 lbs. of sliced baked ham
__ 16 lbs. of red "salad" potatoes
__ 3 lbs. of butter
__ 3 dozen eggs
__ 6 loaves of bread
__ 3+ oz. cans of seasoned bread crumbs
__ 2.5 lbs. of onions
__ 1 jar of peanut butter
__ 1 jar of jelly
__ 1 small box of pancake mix
__ 1 bottle of pancake syrup
__ 2 small bottles of cooking oil
__ 1 small bottle of catsup
__ 1 small bottle of mustard
__ 1 can of mushrooms
__ fish chowder ingredients listed in recipe #6
__ spices and staples
__ 1 39 oz. can of coffee

APPENDICES

Appendix A

SUMMARY CHECKLIST

__ Party Members Chosen
__ Fishing Times and Partners Discussed
__ Vacation Dates Set
__ Information Requested
__ Seasons and Limits Information Received
__ Resort/Outfitter/Charter Reservations Made
__ Request Information from Resort/Outfitter/Charter
__ Deposits Sent
__ Lure/Bait/License Information Received
__ Rod/Reel/Line Recommendations Received
__ Equipment Available Information Received
__ Weight Restriction Information Received (flying)
__ Maps Ordered
__ Transportation Defined
__ Transportation Schedules Received (eg. airline/ferry schedules)
__ Transportation Reservations Made
__ Needed Fishing Equipment Defined
__ Meals Defined
__ Food Purchased
__ Gear and Food Weighed (if necessary)
__ Gear Packed
__ Itinerary Defined and Routed
__ Money Converted

Appendix B

TRIP LOG

Date In _____ Date Out ___
_____

Location _____
_____

Body of Water _____
_____

Party Members _____ Comments ___
_____
_____
_____

Daily Activity
 Date _____
 Moon Phase _____
 Weather:
  Wind _____
  Barometer _____
  General Conditions _____
 Fish Caught Data:
  Specie _____
  Size _____
  Lures/bait _____
  Time _____
  Place _____

INDEX

NOTES

NOTES

NOTES

NOTES

Copies of this book can be ordered from the publisher.

Send $ 7.95 plus $ 1.50 for shipping and handling to:

Barker & North Publishing
P.O. Box 692
Brookfield, Wisconsin   53008-0692

Wisconsin residents add 5% sales tax ($.40)